Contents

Foreword	v
Preface	vii
About the Authors	x
1. Introduction	1
The Importance of Jordan	1
Jordanian Stability	3
Jordanian Tribes in Social Change	4
Implications of Detribalization	6
2. Jordan: Tribes, Nation, State	8
3. The Jordan Arab Army	18
4. Social Change in Jordan	23
Islamic Civilization and Social Change	23
Social Change as a Necessity in Jordan	26

Social Change in Jordan	29
The Nature of Social Change and Jordanian Tribes	36
5. Stability, Security, and Social Change	**49**
Decline of Tribalism	51
Tribalism vs. Nationalism	53
The Jordan Arab Army: Security in Change	61
6. Conclusion	**66**
Notes	**72**
Bibliography	**90**

Foreword

The quest for peace remains both central and elusive in the Middle East. Yet despite all setbacks and disappointments, no one can safely afford not to look constantly for new diplomatic opportunities because of the region's strategic, economic, and political importance.

Any reversal of the peace process or any conceivable substitute thereto is bound to give Jordan a central role. Jordan, with its large Palestinian component, its administration of the West Bank of the Jordan River before the Israeli occupation of 1967, and its close ties to the population of the West Bank clearly make it the essential, inevitable partner to any diplomatic process. Thus the internal social order of the Hashemite Kingdom of Jordan, its domestic solidity, and its cohesion are matters of the greatest importance. This study by Paul A. Jureidini and R. D. McLaurin is designed to make a significant contribution to an understanding of this subject.

Although the numerically larger part of Jordan's present population is now Palestinian, Jordan is not Palestine; neither its Transjordanian nor its Palestinian citizens regard it as such—nor do the Palestinians in the diaspora.* It is the original population of Jordan that gives the country its basic structure and framework, and this is what the authors have set out to explain.

No one who, like myself, has visited Jordan repeatedly over many years, can fail to notice the country's economic and social progress, its increasingly obvious statehood, and its growing identity as a state and nation. Americans in particular will not fail to comprehend and sympathize with the problem as well as the success with which two peoples—Transjordanian and Palestinian, as well as segments of others—have become interwoven and yet remain distinct. The army has played its traditional, nation-building role, while the tribal structure and its transformation have remained significant factors, as the authors explain. The Hashemite dynasty, however, continues to be the single central element in Jordan. This *Washington Paper* makes a significant contribution to the understanding of this pivotal country, which should make it well worth the reader's while because no peace is possible in the Middle East without Jordan.

                    Robert G. Neumann
                    Senior Adviser and
                    Director of Middle East Programs
                    Former U.S. Ambassador
                        to Afghanistan, Morocco, and
                        Saudi Arabia

---

*A different point of view was presented in a previous *Washington Paper,* no. 83, by A. S. Kleiman, *Israel, Jordan, Palestine: The Search for a Durable Peace.*

Preface

The Hashemite Kingdom of Jordan is a small country that has importance well beyond its relative size. Its significance in the Middle East stems from its stability in a turbulent region, its moderation in the face of extremist rhetoric and behavior, its traditional Western orientation in an area often hostile to the West, and, particularly, to the central role of Jordan—both actual and potential—in the course and possible resolution of the Arab-Israeli conflict.

Jordan has been viewed by most analysts as the classic example of a Middle Eastern tribal state. The major tribes and tribal confederations formed the foundation on which the Jordanian government was built and the nucleus of the Jordan Arab Army that first enforced support for that government, and later ensured its stability. As a result of powerful forces of social and economic change, the importance of tribal consciousness is waning. Given the critical role the army plays and the centrality of tribal support in the security of the Hashemite monarchy in the past, what are the implications of these changes for Jordan's future? This paper addresses the impact of social change on Jordanian tribes, with particular reference to their political role in the kingdom.

This study grew out of the authors' extensive research on the political impact of social change in the Middle East, especially in Jordan, Lebanon, and Syria. In the course of this work we have been able to use resources compiled – often somewhat haphazardly – over several years, even though in most cases these data were not originally collected with a view to applying them to this specific study. In addition to printed sources, we have conducted numerous interviews, both in the United States and in Jordan.

We have been extremely fortunate in our work to have had the help of many Jordanians, each of whom was deeply interested in one or more aspects of our research. Virtually every respondent brought some information or insight we did not find in other sources. Those interviewed included sociologists, anthropologists, political scientists, psychologists, military affairs experts, security personnel, present and former cabinet ministers, and Jordanian diplomats. These respondents included persons living both in and outside tribal areas, members of majority and minority religious groups, and residents of Amman and those who live outside Amman. All respondents in the interviews conducted for this paper were educated, however, and all were members of the modern economic sector. For balance, we also considered the views of uneducated and traditional-economy Jordanians to whom we had been exposed over the last few years, although these individuals were not systematically interviewed. Jordan University faculty and Royal Scientific Society staff were particularly helpful. The perspectives gained from our discussions with those individuals and from time spent in Jordan, some of which was devoted to direct contact with the tribes, was of incalculable benefit in the conduct of the research.

Over the years we have benefited from frequent travel to Jordan. At one point, for example, one of the authors met

Jureidini, Paul A.
  Jordan; the impact of social
change on the role of the tribes.
(Washington papers, v.12; 108)
Ctr Strategic & Intl St/Praeger/
CBS Educ & Prof Pub

01 Vol 1984 ISBN 0-03-071853-8

98p

BOOK NO. N8-283590 08-31-84
UNIV OF TULSA
APPROVALS R-527-5
POLI SCI BOOKS

LIST 7.95p

with the leaders of a major tribal alliance that brought together three tribes that reside in an arc sweeping from Iraq to Palestine. He discussed with these leaders the tribal reactions to and perceptions of social change in Jordan, as well as possible future tribal political behavior. Discussions with Crown Prince Hassan bin Talal, whose interest in and devotion to tribal concerns is well known, as well as with other members of the royal family, advisers to the king and crown prince, and government officials have also been invaluable.

The authors have also benefited from the comments of several friends and colleagues. Kamel Abu Jaber and Fawzi Gharaibeh of the Royal Scientific Society have provided especially useful insights. The manuscript was read in its entirety by Peter Gubser (president, American Near East Refugee Aid and author of two books on Jordan), Ronald E. Neumann (U.S. Department of State), Alfred Prados (former U.S. defense attaché, Amman), and Dr. Subhi Utaibeh (Royal Scientific Society), each of whom has commented extensively, generously, and most helpfully. Michael McHenry of the Georgetown University Center for Strategic and International Studies provided detailed and most constructive criticism that has also been very useful. To each of these benefactors we are deeply indebted.

About the Authors

Paul A. Jureidini, vice president of Abbott Associates, Inc., has traveled to Jordan frequently for more than a decade and knows most of the leaders of the kingdom. Dr. Jureidini has worked extensively with the Royal Scientific Society on problems of economic development, social change, and political forecasting. He has also consulted with numerous agencies and departments of the U.S. government, especially as an adviser on the armed forces and societies of Jordan and Lebanon. Dr. Jureidini is the author of a book on Algeria and coauthor of two books on Lebanon and one on the Palestinian movement. He and Dr. McLaurin coauthored a chapter on Jordan in *Lebanon in Crisis*, as well as the book, *Beyond Camp David: Emerging Alignments and Leaders in the Middle East.*

R. D. McLaurin is senior associate at Abbott Associates, Inc. He has also traveled frequently to Jordan and has worked closely with the Royal Scientific Society on political assessments in the Middle East. Dr. McLaurin has consulted widely for private and public sector organizations in the United States and is the author or coauthor of *The Middle East in*

Soviet Policy, Foreign Policy Making in the Middle East, Middle East Foreign Policy: Issues and Processes, The Political Role of Minority Groups in the Middle East, Lebanon and the World in the 1980s, The Emergence of a New Lebanon, and *Beyond Camp David.*

1
Introduction

The Importance of Jordan

The Hashemite Kingdom of Jordan has long played a role in the Middle East far larger than its size and resource base appear to warrant.[1] In part, this position may be due to the political sagacity and sensitivity of King Hussein bin Talal, monarch since 1953, who has reigned through civil and international wars and assassination and coup attempts to establish himself as the regional ruler with the longest uninterrupted tenure since World War II. Yet, in large part, Jordan's importance transcends Hussein and derives from the country's location and political climate.

Jordan is at the heart of the Palestinian dilemma — more than any other Arab state its life cannot be separated from the history, course, and future of the Arab-Israeli problem. The 1948 occupation by Transjordanian forces of parts of Palestine west of the Jordan River, King Abdullah's annexation of that territory — changing Transjordan, the "land across the Jordan," into Jordan — and the general acquiescence in that annexation created a powerful link between

Palestine and Jordan. This bond has since manifested itself in some of the most prominent Arab-Israeli settlement ideas, which feature some organic link between a "Palestinian" political entity on the West Bank and Jordan (Transjordan), in disputes over who "represents" the Palestinian people, and in reminders from some quarters that "there already is a Palestinian state—its name is Jordan."[2]

Even beyond the central position Jordan occupies in the Palestinian problem and the Arab-Israeli conflict, the country's importance also results from its situation as a buffer between the Levant, or Eastern Mediterranean part of the Arab world, on the one hand, and the Gulf subregion, on the other. Over the years U.S. policy endeavored to insulate the two subregions from each other, and Jordan fit into this policy well by participating actively, but quite differently, in both areas.[3] Changes in the military and political balances within the Middle East have increased the perceived importance of Jordan's Gulf role to U.S. policymakers.[4]

Moreover, Jordan has been one of the few relatively stable factors in a turbulent region. Whether in the 1960s, the 1970s, or today, the end of the political stability of the Jordanian monarchy could have far-reaching and very adverse effects on regional security. And, as the stability of Jordan was recognized and accepted by other regional powers—in some cases, reluctantly—the country's influence grew. The leadership has also behaved with a rhetorical and diplomatic moderation uncharacteristic of the Middle East. This moderation has been particularly consonant with general U.S. foreign policy objectives, even when Amman and Washington pursued conflicting short-term paths. Jordan's moderate approach to foreign—and, to a great extent, domestic—policy has facilitated the opening of channels of communication between Jordan's neighbors and powers outside the region (including the United States).

Jordanian Stability

Jordan's political stability does not derive from homogeneity, wealth, or regional military power. Although the kingdom is not torn by as many types of subnational loyalty problems as Lebanon or Syria, its population is far from homogeneous.[5] "Jordanians" — those whose families are tied to the East Bank or who came from the Arabian Peninsula in the 1920s after the House of Hashem was defeated by the House of Sa'ud — are a minority in the country, outnumbered by "Palestinians" (those whose family base is west of the Jordan).[6] There are also conflicts between the urbanized and the less urbanized and among various tribes or leading families. Christians play a role in business and government out of proportion to their numbers and, as the current cycle of Islamic consciousness grips Jordan more and more firmly, some sectarian strains are also in evidence.

Nor does the kingdom have great resources with which to co-opt its challengers. Despite numerous explorations, oil has only recently been found, but in meager quantities. Much of the land is arid, and minerals are scarcely more abundant than water. Hundreds of thousands of Jordanians, however, including Palestinians now residing in Jordan, are benefiting from the wealth of the Gulf oil economies by working as skilled and unskilled labor in Gulf nations.[7] Their remittances are a major source of income for Jordan.

In Middle Eastern terms, Jordan's armed forces are neither large nor well armed.[8] Confronting Israel on the west, Syria to the north, and Iraq on the east, Jordan's military appears relatively small and lightly equipped, although the kingdom's military forces are often considered the best, on a man-for-man basis, in the Middle East.[9] The Jordan Arab Army has proved quite capable of maintaining internal security under all but the most unusual circumstances, and it is supported by an intelligence organization that some observers believe is the best in the Arab world.[10]

Jordan's stability has not depended principally upon force, however. Rather, it has been based on the genuine popularity of the king and traditional support for the monarchy. Accounts of Hussein's popularity in Jordan are legion, and if the monarchy itself has enjoyed only slightly less support, still the bedouin traditions underlying the Hashemite Kingdom and its institutions are strong. Whether a true "Jordanian" nationalism exists even today may be doubted by some and the question is treated subsequently in this paper. There is no doubt, however, that over the years tribal loyalties have been a much more powerful focal point of identification and action than loyalties to the state.

In the early years of the kingdom (and to some extent to this day) it was the ability of the king—Abdullah, Talal, and now Hussein—to marshal and exploit the tribal loyalties that guaranteed Jordan's stability. The Jordan Arab Army, a direct successor to Sir John Bagot Glubb's (Glubb Pasha) "Arab Legion," has always been infused with loyalty based upon tribal support of the monarch.[11] And today the politics of Jordan revolve around the monarchy's handling of competing families and tribes, as they have for a half-century.

Jordanian Tribes in Social Change

Thus the stability of Jordan has rested on the tribal nature of politics and social relations in the kingdom. The social change that is sweeping the Middle East is affecting the role of tribes in Jordanian life, however.

Detribalization is the process by which the role of the tribe in an individual's sense of personal identification and living patterns declines. This process has been under way in Jordan for many years as a function of urbanization, government settlement policies, and the growth of Jordanian nationalism, education, and other modernizing factors.

Urbanization is clearly an important force in contemporary Jordan, and a substantial proportion of the population resides in four cities—Amman, the capital; Salt; Zarqa; and Irbid. A fifth city, Ramtha, is also a major population center. Zarqa has grown very rapidly and is the center of a large industrial boom. As Jordan's economy is affected increasingly by the dynamic financial developments in the Gulf and by the kingdom's role as a marginal political and economic interface, urbanizing pressures will grow apace.

Moreover, for some years the government has actively pursued policies to settle or resettle various nomadic tribes.[12] Both the Three-Year Development Plan (1973-1975) and the recent Five-Year Plan (1976-1980) were drafted with great concern for tribal welfare and the integration of the bedouin into the modern economy.[13] Official settlement policies have had a marked effect on most of the major nomadic tribes.

Jordanian nationalism—slow to develop because of the complete absence of any historic roots of a Jordanian "nation," the nature of the government's relationship to the people in the kingdom, the sudden influxes of Palestinian refugees, and the ambivalence of the monarchy itself concerning the nature of Jordanian identity—has finally begun to develop in the cities and among Jordan's elites.[14] Loyalties based on state nationalism differ fundamentally from both internal tribal loyalties and collective tribal loyalties to the monarchy.

The spread of education has cut deeply into tribal traditions. Even among the nomadic bedouin, the vast majority (more than 80 percent) of males age 15 to 19 has had some education, and a slight majority has gone beyond primary to preparatory and secondary education.[15] Education tends to awaken broader social awareness and thereby proliferate the foci of social identification. It is believed by many—including the royal family—that this process has already progressed far in Jordan.

Implications of Detribalization

If indications of the diminution of the tribal role in Jordanian society are valid—and there are contradictory signs, as well—such a change poses major challenges to the Jordanian monarchy in terms of security, stability, and political development.[16]

Behind the popularity of the king has always been the unquestioned loyalty of the Jordan Arab Army, based on tribal fidelity to the monarch. Would a nontribal army, or one in which tribal loyalties constituted a less compelling motivation, be as dependable?

Control of the armed forces and key political support at the national level have depended upon allocation of important positions and "opportunities" to members of leading tribes and families. To the extent that tribal power wanes, less security will result from such appointments. Similarly, as other power centers develop, there will be less incentive on the part of the monarchy to satisfy the ambitions and appetites of the leading families and tribes. Such changes are destabilizing.

Internal security (intelligence) and other sensitive functions continue to be allocated by and are dependent on tribal affiliations and loyalties. The Jordanian internal security apparatus is highly regarded in the Middle East, and a deterioration in tribal loyalties to the monarch—or vice versa— as a result of social change could have serious implications for the capacity of the internal security network to function effectively.[17]

Although the nature of King Hussein's popularity among Jordanians certainly transcends mere tribal loyalty, there is little question that significant discontinuities in established patterns of allocation of national resources and power may endanger the stability of the government by escalating aggregate expectations in a society whose resources are tightly constrained.

Finally, although Jordan is a constitutional monarchy, the country's political culture has granted the king and royal family a virtually free hand in most administrative areas, from foreign policy and economic development to science and technology investments. This executive freedom suited the traditional Jordanian approach to government, based on assured support from key tribes as the necessary and sufficient lowest common denominator of security. Such freedom is less appropriate to a more broadly based political substructure, which would probably not tolerate it. In fact, since the death of his uncle, Sherif Nasir, King Hussein has been presented with several urgent "requests" for policy decisions by consensus (meaning consultation with tribal leaders). Although these appeals have come from the leading families, they may represent a dilution of the fealty the monarchy once enjoyed and therefore may constitute a precursor to broader claims for participation. It is not at all clear that the personalities, traditions, or institutions of the kingdom could easily adapt to such a change.

This paper is an assessment of the impact of changes in the nature of the tribal role in Jordan on the country's political institutions and processes. The chapters consist of a brief historical overview, a discussion of the traditional role of Jordanian tribes, an examination of the processes of the continuing social changes that affect that role, and finally, an analysis of the impact of these changes on Jordanian politics and the prospects for stability in the kingdom.

2

Jordan: Tribes, Nation, State

The history of the Hashemite Kingdom of Jordan is short – just over 30 years. Its predecessor, Transjordan, existed for even fewer years. Indeed, the concept of a modern state in the general area now occupied by Jordan was born as recently as the 1920s, far more a function of chance than of design. It would be incorrect to infer that areas west and east of the Jordan River were unoccupied until after World War I, misleading to suggest the area had little earlier history, and dangerous to overlook the fundamental imprint that early inhabitants and culture have left on Jordan. Yet, the historical relationship between earlier inhabitants and those of the present has been affected by several cataclysmic developments.

Both the East and West Banks of the Jordan River have been populated for millennia – archaeological evidence suggests sedentary settlements on both banks of the river as early as 10 thousand years ago. From that time to the present, the area has been continuously inhabited. Over the several thousand years before the current century, the area west of the Jordan became known as Palestine, characterized by a largely urban civilization and populated by Arabs.[18] East of the Jordan, apart from a few small towns on the river itself and leaving aside the Crusader settlements (later absorbed by the Arab population), there was little sedentary population.[19] The dominant form of social organization was that of the tribe, and nomadic bedouin tribes were scarcely controlled by the nominal sovereign, whether the Romans or the Ottomans. The histories of the two sides of the Jordan, then, are extensive and rather divergent—by the start of the twentieth century, although both were predominantly Arab (almost entirely Arab east of the river), the West Bank was dominated by an urban culture, while the East Bank remained heavily nomadic or seminomadic and sparsely settled.[20]

The less settled and Islamic character of the East Bank contrasted sharply and increasingly with the urban and multireligious (though still predominantly Muslim) West Bank, and the greater influence of the West and the presence of a large Christian minority accentuated this contrast. Palestine's interactions were to the north and west after the advent of the Ottomans; those of the East Bank were essentially to the south in the Arabian desert.[21]

This was the situation as war enveloped Europe and the Ottoman Empire in 1914. Meanwhile, a growing Arab consciousness in the nineteenth and early twentieth centuries had resulted in the conception of an embryonic Arab nationalism. In 1916, the Hashemites, led by Sherif Hussein, the guardian of Mecca and ruler of the Hijaz, joined forces with the British to spark the so-called Arab Revolt against Ottoman rule.[22] Working with several British agents and military personnel, two of Hussein's sons, Faisal and Abdullah, waged what amounted to guerrilla warfare against the Ottomans, with a view to securing an independent pan-Arab state after the war. Sherif Hussein was concerned about the Balfour Declaration and other pledges to Zionist groups, but he believed that an Arab state led by the Hashemites would, in fact, become a reality based upon the Arab war for independence (as he saw the Arab Revolt) and would be supported by the British after the war.[23]

Ottoman territories did not achieve independence, however. Instead, their boundaries were redrawn and they were placed under the League of Nations mandate system as class A mandates. Palestine and the land east of the Jordan River – still nameless – were placed together in a single mandate under the authority of the United Kingdom.[24]

This period is particularly interesting, but is not particularly well documented. It has given rise to an important controversy about the legitimacy of a distinct Jordanian entity. On the one hand, some have alleged that the British mandatory authority "illegally" partitioned the mandate, dividing a land – Palestine – given in its entirety to the United Kingdom as a mandate to create a Jewish national home.

On the other hand, there are those who insist that this allegedly illegal partitioning proves that Jordan is in fact part of Palestine and therefore should be or is a Palestinian state. Jordan and Palestine are distinct historically, geographically, and socially, but the distinction between the two has been blurred by external factors past and present. A major difficulty is that the name, "Palestine," like "America," has had several meanings over the centuries, referring to a general geographic area as well as to a specific jurisdiction. Nevertheless, both anthropologically and politically, Palestine as a specific term has always referred to the coastal areas, originally settled by peoples of Cretan origin around the twelfth century B.C. Although these coastal peoples were Arabized during the Arab conquest of the region, they remained a settled, agrarian society. By contrast, nomadic bedouin of purer Arab stock predominated on the East Bank. The distinction between nomadic pastoralists and settled cultivators, one of the most basic in human society, remained generally applicable to East and West Bank civilization until well into the twentieth century.

Thus, two distinct and disparate territories and two peoples whose common heritage was virtually limited to the Arabic language were thrown together, although some tribal and even nomadic elements remained on the West Bank and some towns existed on the East Bank. Moreover, in many cases the same tribe had East and West Bank branches—especially true of some tribes around Salt and Karak. The union of Palestine and the area to the east was brief, because in 1921 Britain, the future mandatory power, unilaterally divided the territory into two parts, separated by the Jordan River. In practice, no union had taken place, for the land east of the Jordan was seen by the British as a desert, unsettled and ungoverned. From 1920 on, the British government appears to have planned that, although a unified civil administration was to be established in Palestine, the region east of the Jordan would be governed by several local administrations based in a few major towns such as Karak, Salt, and Irbid.[25]

In a sense, the actual establishment of Jordan is linked at least as much to Syria, Iraq, and what is today Saudi Arabia as it is to Palestine. If northern "Jordan" was part of geographical Syria, the southern part of the country was definitely part of the Hijaz. During and at the end of World War I, Sherif Hussein's son Faisal governed "Syria," including today's Lebanon and northern Jordan. His rule was sanctioned by the Allied occupation authority, and his government, based in Damascus, was effective in varying degrees over much of the territory. Pursuant to the Sykes-Picot agreement secretly concluded between the British and French during the war, however, France was assigned the mandate for a "Syria" much reduced in size, a Syria corresponding to something like present-day Syria and Lebanon.[26] Thus, although Faisal had since been proclaimed king of a "greater" Syria including Palestine by the General Syrian Congress, French forces attacked and removed Faisal's forces in July 1920. (Faisal was later made king of Iraq.)

Meanwhile, Abdullah, purporting to plan, organize, and carry out a rebellion against the French to restore Syria to Hashemite control, left Mecca in October 1920 by train. He arrived at Ma'an on November 11, where he announced he was regent (for Faisal), declared a *jihad* (holy war) against the French, and reaffirmed his intention to oust the French from Syria.[27] (Ma'an, today well inside Jordan, was then considered part of the Hijaz.) In Ma'an, he met with the British resident, and four months later he left Ma'an for Amman, arriving on March 2, 1921. At the end of March Abdullah met with then-Colonial Secretary Winston Churchill, reaching an agreement that in effect gave British backing to a government under Abdullah in the land east of the Jordan, providing that this government would in turn follow the direction of a British resident.[28] The precise frontiers of this land were not determined.

The new government got off to a rapid administrative start, establishing its basic laws on April 27, 1921. Jordan's creation may therefore be realistically viewed as the spring of 1921, because, even though its borders were still unclear, a concept of a unified state south and exclusive of Syria, west of Iraq, east and exclusive of Palestine, and north of the Arabian Peninsula emerged. This area became known as Transjordan.

A static recounting of events may suffice to portray the legal or institutional history of Jordan. It is inadequate for present purposes, however, because this layer of institutions does not reflect either the most important aspects of what was taking place in the area or the true relationship of government institutions to the people. In reality, existing social dynamics continued to dominate Transjordan, and these dynamics were based on a tribal social structure that reached even into the towns. In the north, around Irbid and Salt, tribal life had already progressed to the extent that most residents were sedentary. Under these circumstances, tribal social organization was already giving way to extended family structures. But for identity and certain authority issues, the tribes remained the principal reference group, and family or clan structures were never far removed from their tribal base.[29]

Political scientists and geographers often make the error of looking at human social organization in exclusively spatial terms. We shall discuss this concept more fully in chapter 4, but it is important to recognize here that tribal movements were extensive and were the essence of, rather than the exception to, regional history. Migration was caused by climate and the physical changes wrought by climate, by changing power alliances, and by successive tribal surges over the centuries northward from the southern Arabian Peninsula.

During the 1910s and 1920s large-scale tribal migrations surpassing the norm were also a major element in transforming the area. These movements resulted from a variety of factors, but many affecting Transjordan were associated with the Wahhabi attacks on Hashemite supremacy in Arabia.[30] Tribal raids, feuds, counterraids, and tribally based alignments were central political, economic, and social realities of Transjordan. Few tribesmen, and even relatively few of the settled population in the principal towns—Salt, Irbid, Karak, and Amman—paid any attention to, or were aware of, the role of the British, the nature of the mandate, or the intentions of Abdullah to govern Transjordan.

It must be understood that villages and to some extent towns were largely an outgrowth of the tribal substructure. The "settled" populations, and particularly the peasants or *fellahin*, were traditionally held in contempt by nomadic bedouin as degenerate and weak. Bedouin values were associated with behavior (such as raiding) characteristic of mobile armed groups, but were values no longer appropriate for those who had settled. Consequently, despite common origins, bedouin disdained the settled. During some periods, foreign non-Arab suzerains succeeded in imposing some degree of security in order to exploit the villages. Invariably, however, these protectors eventually left, taking with them protection against the nomadic tribes. At this point, and until the next wave of foreign control imposed itself, the nomads usually dominated the village, a local tribe receiving "protection" payments that ensured only against raids of that local tribe.[31] Despite the fundamental social division (settled vs. nomads), urban society was also based on kinship, and both the *fellahin* and bedouin were tribal.[32]

The governments in the Middle East have opposed nomadism. At its heart, nomadic movements contravene the raison d'être of the state — security. Tribes have recognized no "international" boundaries, and have ignored them. Tribes from Syria, Transjordan, and the Arabian Peninsula have regularly entered the territory of other states, raided other bedouin encampments, and moved on. For these and other reasons many Middle Eastern governments (as well as others affected by nomadism) have adopted plans and procedures to settle their nomads forcibly.

Although Transjordan faced many of the same problems confronted by other countries with nomadic populations, Abdullah did not support the forcible sedentarization of the bedouin. He was concerned about, and took effective steps to curtail, bedouin raiding, but, perhaps because he identified with the bedouin to a large extent, Abdullah opposed compulsory measures to settle, much less resettle, Jordan's nomads.[33]

This does not mean that Abdullah intended to accept either nomadism or border crossing as inviolable rituals, nor does it mean that he failed to perceive the problems that these activities generated for Transjordan. On the contrary, he determined to alter bedouin behavior by providing incentives rather than disincentives. Abdullah began to regularize and codify bedouin customary law as early as 1924, an effort that involved the government of Transjordan in what had been purely tribal business. In 1929, he initiated the first legislative attempts at control over the tribes with the Bedouin Control Law.[34]

The sedentarization process in Transjordan was also aided by the fact that most of the tribes lived near or between villages from the inception of the state.[35] Thus, the adjustment to a settled life was evolutionary. Moreover, as effective civil administration took hold under Transjordanian government, tribal leaders were consulted regularly. To the extent they were involved in local administrative matters, residence in or near a village or town and its communication and transportation facilities became increasingly important and desirable.[36]

In spite of the incentives offered for settlement, the process consumed about five decades in addition to the period before establishment of the mandate during which sedentarization actually began. Tribal settlement was largely complete by 1960, with nomadic populations less than 10 percent of the total population of the East Bank. The bedouin heritage has not been relegated to the past, however, and no visitor to the country can fail to be impressed by the continuing pride taken in the Jordanian bedouin tradition.

Tribal society, bedouin heritage, and social evolution might well have been the dominant themes of Jordanian history except for events across the Jordan River. As early as 1936, Transjordan was affected by the growing violence in Palestine, and, if Jordan was an unwilling victim of the complex problem in Palestine, its victimization was to grow rather than diminish.[37]

> From 1932 to 1948 the whole of Jordan was indeed one of the happiest little countries in the world. In spite of poverty and drought, in spite of troubles and upheavals

in neighboring countries, in spite even of a world war, Trans-Jordan seemed to lead a charmed life. The people acquired an almost superstitious confidence – and a fond pride – in the happiness of their country. With the rest of the world in agony, with the neighboring Arab countries in constant upheaval, in Trans-Jordan for sixteen years nothing could go wrong.... "We were so happy until 1948."[38]

It will never be possible to know what might have been Jordan's future had the first Arab-Israeli war not occurred in 1948-1949, for the history of Jordan and that of the Palestinian Arabs have been indissolubly linked ever since. Beyond the Arab-Israeli wars in which Jordan has participated, beyond the civil war of 1970-1971 and the cross-border violence, beyond the implications of the arms spending required by the conflict with Israel, beyond Amman's annexation and loss of the West Bank, and beyond the constant political pressure for 30 years concerning Jordan's role in a future settlement with Israel is the overriding, boundless, and immeasurable impact of the influx of Palestinians since 1948 on the people and society of Jordan, on this small, poor, but "happy" country.

The influx of Palestinians was not limited to 1948-1949, but continued from 1948 until the mid-1950s, then recurred in 1967.[39] This was a population change in numbers greater than the total population of Jordan in 1948 – and a population whose circumstances and way of life contrasted sharply with those of the people of Transjordan. It is safe to say that no event in Jordan's history – neither independence nor the advent of the British nor the assassination of King Abdullah (which, like virtually all major events since 1948, was directly linked to the Palestine problem) – has been nearly as profound in its impact on Jordanian life.

Transjordan participated in the war of 1948-1949, and,

as a result, the West Bank, including East Jerusalem, was annexed to the kingdom, resulting in a change of name to the Hashemite Kingdom of Jordan. King Abdullah, Jordan's founder, a wise monarch with a deep and abiding faith in his people and in his own mission who had watched Jordan develop very much in the direction he had hoped, was assassinated in Jerusalem in 1951 in the presence of his grandson Prince Hussein, whom Abdullah had clearly been grooming for the throne and to whom he was extremely close.[40] Abdullah was succeeded, after a brief interlude, by his eldest son, Talal, who abdicated in favor of *his* eldest son, Prince Hussein, about one year later, and Hussein, Jordan's ruler, was crowned in May 1953.[41]

3

The Jordan Arab Army

The military situation in Transjordan at the end of World War I was no more stable than the political situation described in the preceding chapter. The Ottoman government had been defeated, although some Ottoman-appointed police remained more or less on duty, albeit without pay, in the area east of the Jordan. The Syrian Arab government had sent some officials and security forces south to the area, and Sherif Hussein had also sent some government officials to parts of the same area. Furthermore, local governments of more or less independent origin erupted in the north, while tribal power reasserted itself in the south.[42] Disorder was rampant.

The British government inserted itself into this chaotic situation. Still undecided about what to do with the area, the British recognized that order had to be restored. Captain Frederick G. Peake of the Egyptian Camel Corps reported on the situation, recommended the formation of a "reserve force" to buttress local police (at least in the towns in which British officers were living and along the Amman-Palestine road), and, upon receiving permission from his military superiors, established the force.[43]

Soon after the first deployments of the reserve force, Abdullah arrived in Ma'an with approximately 200 infantry.[44] Abdullah had been given the mandatory power's sanction to assume authority over the entire area in an agreement with Churchill on March 29, 1921, and one of his first efforts was the establishment of a coherent security force that would ensure his control of the entire mandated territory east of the River Jordan.[45] After several unsuccessful initiatives and at least one major tribal rebellion, Abdullah secured a promise from the British government to support a military force of 750 men.[46] Officers of the reserve force, which was the predecessor of the Jordan Arab Army, were Arabs from the Ottoman army and Egypt, and virtually all the soldiers were Arabs from outside the area. The principal activities of the reserve force were control of tribal rebellions, defense against Wahhabi raids from the south, and tax collection.[47]

In 1923, all security forces in the territory were combined into the Arab Legion (the usual English name for *al-jaysh al-'arabi*) under Peake's command.[48] In 1926, the British High Commission for Palestine established for external security purposes the Transjordan Frontier Force (TJFF), which reported to the high commissioner rather than to Abdullah, leaving the Arab Legion primarily to police functions and reducing its size by about half.[49] The TJFF was never as successful as the original Arab Legion-Royal Air Force (RAF) combination had been in defending Transjordan's borders, and the depleted Arab Legion was inadequate to prevent tribal raids and uprisings.[50] Thus, in 1930, Captain John Glubb, who had spent the previous decade dealing with Iraqi bedouin tribes, was detailed to Transjordan. There, ostensibly Peake's deputy, he organized the Desert Mobile Force, which was to become the heart of the strike force of the Arab Legion and, later, the Jordan Arab Army.[51]

The Arab Legion grew with the increasing problems in Palestine, then again during World War II (in which it conducted limited but effective operations), and was reorganized on the eve of the withdrawal of the British from Palestine (which was, in effect, the beginning of the first Arab-Israeli war), after which it increased again.[52]

The Jordan Arab Army is significant because of its central role in the evolution and development of Jordan and for its relationship to the tribal structure of the Transjordan society. Although Transjordan's original security forces were established under Peake to maintain and enforce the authority of Abdullah, the concept behind those forces was largely conventional. Unusual hurdles confronted Peake (and Abdullah) in unifying Transjordan, in establishing the authority of a central government based in what was the small town of Amman, and in controlling the disparate elements within the Legion, which, as we have indicated, were recruited from local remnants of the Ottoman army, along with Egyptians and Arabs from other nearby countries, including Palestinians. Some of these Arab personnel were Syrian officers whose principal objective was to oust the French from Syria, and they and their compatriots created continual problems between Transjordan and the French mandatory authority in Syria.[53] Yet perhaps the major challenge was control of the bedouin tribes, which continued to raid each other and, to a much lesser extent, the villages, paying no attention to the new and arbitrary international borders that cut across their traditional migratory areas.[54]

It was Glubb who succeeded in addressing this problem. Fresh from dealing with similar difficulties in Iraq, Glubb organized his Desert Mobile Force composed largely of bedouin elements. The bedouin and other tribal groups had traditionally viewed the government and the armed forces as hostile – and with reason.[55] Glubb's personal triumph was to demonstrate the value of the new force to the bedouin, especially to the major tribes, as well as to others.[56] He appealed to each tribe or group on the basis of its own interests. All initially feared that the Desert Mobile Force would be used in favor of the settled populations and against them. Their fears were put to rest through the personality of Glubb and the activities of the force—including the willingness of the force to defend Transjordanians against attacks by non-Transjordanians such as the Arabian Wahhabis and against attacks by other tribes within Transjordan. Tribal leaders became concerned instead with achieving great *enough* representation on the Desert Force to ensure that it not be dominated by hostile tribes.[57]

The Huwaytat was the first major Transjordanian tribe to succumb to Glubb's blandishments and became the backbone of the Desert Mobile Force. Until very recently the Huwaytat have provided a large proportion of the army's bedouin manpower. Other major bedouin tribes also have participated heavily, however—such as the Bani Sakhr, the Sirhan, the Shammar, and the Bani Hassan. In general, the Arab Legion's Desert Mobile Force was heavily manned by southern tribes until World War II, when more northern tribes, both settled and bedouin, began to join the Legion.[58]

Gradually, Glubb assumed a greater role in the army than merely that of Peake's deputy. The bedouin, principal stock of the Desert Mobile Force, became an increasingly prominent element of the army as a whole, eventually forming the bulk of its officer corps and strike units. In 1939, Glubb succeeded Peake as commander of the army, a post he retained until he was dismissed by King Hussein in 1956. Peake and many of his contemporaries had serious doubts about the wisdom of basing the army on tribal bedouin.[59] Glubb, however, saw major advantages and translated these potential benefits into real ones. Glubb, and many others, felt that the warrior tradition of the bedouin, his avowed loyalty and pride, willingness to sacrifice, and ability to live and fight in conditions of hardship were important attributes of any army serving in this part of the Middle East. Until the

1970s, the Jordan Arab Army was essentially a tribal army, a force based on and reflecting the social structure of what were once the major bedouin tribes. Recruitment for the Desert Mobile Force and, later, for the Arab Legion, was consciously designed to reflect rather than alter existing tribal social structure. Sons of tribal shaykhs were expected to become officers and would not be subordinate to the sons of the unranking tribal membership, because such a reversal of social roles would have created unsettling reactions within the tribes. Even now, the senior officer corps clearly traces its roots to this same heritage. But both the officer corps and especially the army as a whole beneath the senior levels have begun to reflect a very different composition.

4

Social Change in Jordan

Since the establishment of the Hashemite Kingdom of Jordan, the country's rulers, Abdullah and Hussein, have been committed to social change, but the nature of this desired change must be understood in the context of regional dynamics and national realities. (The rule of King Talal was brief and is therefore difficult to characterize.)

Islamic Civilization and Social Change

Western observers of the Muslim world perceive that world as a stagnant society. They believe that its rulers are hostile to social change, and the appeals of socialism and similar policies of rapid change appear foreign and contrary to the mass conservative instincts that are powerfully reinforced by Islamic culture. Such philosophies are seen to be imposed from above or promoted by various elites. To the extent that a positive popular response arises, Western observers may be aware of the critical socializing role of the mass media and the seductive attractions of the material benefits of industrialized life. Although these perspectives have some validity, they are at best only partially relevant and fundamentally misconstrue the nature of change in Muslim lands.

Social change has certainly been perceived as a threat by some traditional leadership elites. Several of the smaller Gulf states' rulers, as well as a number of Saudi leaders, were reticent about change for years and attempted to prevent it, rather than trying to monitor and regulate its nature, direction, and velocity. Many who believed that change was inevitable mocked these "backward" potentates both for their efforts to prevent change and for their fears of it. History may suggest that the critics were correct about the futility of trying to prevent change, but it is not at all clear that the rulers' fears were groundless.

Islamic groups in Egypt and Jordan continue to oppose key elements of what the governments see as modernization but religious groups perceive to be "Westernization" and, as such, a threat to the Muslim community. Political leaders in both countries seek a way to compromise. American visitors to Jordan can watch hours of religious sermons, Koran reading, and other religiously-oriented programming on Jordanian television.

Social change is not an inherent and fundamental element of Islam.[60] Although the religion anticipates individual efforts to modify one's behavior in the direction of social good, the concepts of "progress" and the assumption that forces of change are indeed "progressive" (i.e., moving "forward" toward a better "good") are not as closely associated with Islamic cultural perspectives as they are with some Western religions.[61] It is also true that much of the concept of and an impulse toward social change, which are not inherent in Islamic countries, can be directly associated with the interaction of those countries with the West.

Where the traditional observations are seriously in error is in the interstices of these two essentially correct points of departure. Western civilization is seen as hostile, as a challenge to Islam and to Muslim civilization. Thus, it is incorrect to see the modernizing impulse as an accepted Westernizing impulse. Quite to the contrary, there have been a range of reactions to the Western challenge, some totally hostile and basically oriented toward a "return" to the strength of the past, some totally hostile yet oriented toward a revolutionary rejection of past and present, with others between the two extremes. The first may be exemplified by Iran. An equally clear example of the second—a wholly secular, revolutionary state—has not emerged on the national level, although the People's Democratic Republic of Yemen (PDRY) may be nominally close to such an example. (Of course, the PDRY is much more a tribal than a revolutionary society.)

A middle approach between the extremes that embrace most Arab states today is characterized by less overt hostility and an orientation toward learning from the West and toward adopting the tools of the West so that Islamic civilization might triumph in the end.[62] What is critical and often missed by the outside observer is that the fundamental objective is not pro-Western. Indeed, it is hostile to the West—it continues to regard the West as a challenge, a threat to Islam. We are not arguing that individuals can be characterized in this manner. Often, those who are the vehicles of this "moderate" approach are themselves so secularized or so Westernized as to have rejected many elements of their own culture. But to be acceptable to the Islamic mainstream, cooperation with the West, the tolerance of Western innovations and presence, and the reformist or modernizing initiatives must be perceived by that mainstream as a means to enable the *dar al-Islam*—the Islamic world—to overcome Western "inroads." Leaders such as King Hussein and the late Anwar Sadat have ensured the presence of a strong Islamic base underneath their cooperation with the West. They have worked diligently to preserve their credibility as devout Muslim leaders, however secular specific programs or initiatives may have appeared.[63]

King Hussein has always carried religious legitimacy by claiming descent from the Prophet Muhammad and has exploited this legitimacy as necessary. Sadat, long deeply involved in religious activities in Egypt, worked hard to retain his reputation as a devout Muslim. He was widely believed to have helped spread the impression that the dark spot on his forehead resulted from praying five times daily (one of the obligations of Islam). Still, criticism of Sadat grew as the Western presence in Egypt grew, and the most powerful critics were not those of the Left, who had no real constituency, but rather the Islamic Right, which based itself on the conservatism of the Egyptian population and Muslim culture. His close association with the West, especially with the United States, the Western orientation of his policies, and his attempts to modernize personal status laws and other aspects of society especially provoked religious critics.

Even beyond the Islamic dimension, Jordan has been particularly successful in adapting – not just adopting – Western approaches to suit the particular circumstances of Jordan. The concept of legitimacy is frequently used by political scientists to describe a leader, an elite, or a system of government, although this concept can usefully be applied to governmental behavior as an element of, not merely a result of, leadership legitimacy. Adaptive behavior bolsters system legitimacy, as compared with adoptive behavior, which may undermine legitimacy.

Social Change as a Necessity in Jordan

We leave what may seem a somewhat abstruse consideration to address a more pragmatic one. The interests of modern Jordan in the second half of the twentieth century, more than those of any other major Arab state, have required a specific type of social change. The other major Arab states, however weak their national identities, have all had some political tradition on which to draw in attempting to develop modern nationalistic support: Iraqis could look back to the Abbasids, Syrians to the Umayyads. If Saudi Arabia is a relatively new political entity, there is still a Saudi pride in their role as guardians of the holy cities and as the fount of much original Arab culture. Egypt, alone among the Arab states, can point to thousands of years of a distinctly Egyptian heritage. Algeria, Morocco, and Tunisia have all had extensive traditions as separate entities with clear histories.[64] Only Libya challenges Jordan in its absence of a quasi-national tradition, the various parts of the country being unified only after World War II.

From the time of Abdullah's arrival in the "area east of the Jordan" in 1920, one of his principal objectives was to build a state and construct a national—and personal—allegiance where none had been. For this reason, it may be argued that planned social change has been a constant feature of Jordanian national policy. The struggle to create loyalties to Transjordan (or, later, Jordan), or even to create narrower loyalties to its Hashemite rulers, found substantial challenges and inevitably meant the eventual superimposition of national loyalties on tribal loyalties.

The Hashemite kings could have been content with the long-term objective of building a national consciousness had there been no challenges to their rule. Because they were intensely sensitive to the fact that the land east of the Jordan did not exist in a political vacuum, Abdullah and Hussein recognized the need to deal with potential internal opposition and external challenges long before the ultimate objective could be reached. In Abdullah's case, early Wahhabi expansionist moves tested Transjordan, and the challenge of unifying the disparate elements of the country and codifying its administrative and political direction consumed many years. As Transjordan began to take shape, the problems of Palestine spilled across the river and preempted much of Abdullah's effort. Nevertheless, his success in creating a state gave purpose and direction both to internal and external enemies who now had something to oppose, a problem with which King Hussein has been preoccupied. Transjordan took its place in the state system of the Middle East, with all of the complications of coalition politics and the dynamics of cooperation and conflict that that implies. Hussein has faced infinitely more challenges to his rule—both internal and external—than did his grandfather and for the last two decades has not had the implied or formal protection of the United Kingdom, which may have deterred many of Abdullah's potential opponents.[65]

In the short term, therefore, Abdullah and Hussein recognized that they had to depend upon tribal loyalties, and both have profited immensely from their closeness to the bedouin tribes of Jordan, looking to tribal support as the internal guarantor of Hashemite control. Yet, both understood that some sense of "Jordanianism" must eventually grow if the monarchy were to survive, for Jordan itself would be an ephemeral phenomenon without it.

Moreover, the "crisis" of Western penetration could not be prevented in Jordan any more than elsewhere in the Arab world, especially because Abdullah depended upon British support to establish, protect, and extend his effective domain. Even had this not been the case, the growth of communications and improved transportation still precluded the seclusion of Jordan from such broad cultural realities as Western penetration and domination.[66] Thus the concept of social change that we have broadly described as that of the Arab world certainly affected Jordan and its Hashemite leaders as well.

Social Change in Jordan

Jordan is simplistically characterized by many writers as two societies in one country.[67] The two societies are the "Palestinian" and the "Jordanian." Palestinian means those peoples or groups whose roots may be traced to the land west of the River Jordan, while Jordanian means generally those whose origins are to the east of the river. Beyond the fact that this dichotomy fails to take into account important distinctions among the Palestinians, it is also misleading as regards Jordanians.[68] It ignores such differences as region, sedentarization, religion, socioeconomic status, and education.

Because the authors' purpose is to consider the implications of some aspects of social change on the tribes of Jordan, the subject of the Palestinians will not be discussed except where directly relevant. Even though the West Bank of the Jordan River—territory currently under Israeli occupation—is part of the Hashemite Kingdom of Jordan, there are several reasons to avoid consideration of West Bank tribes still resident there.[69] In addition to the Jordanian government's position since 1974 that the Palestine Liberation Organization (PLO) is the sole legitimate representative of the Palestinian people, the West Bank was never fully integrated into the kingdom before 1967.[70] Indeed, the heritage of tribal support for Abdullah is clearly an East Bank phenomenon, and the relationship of the Hashemites to the West Bank, even including the special situation of Jerusalem (which, in any event, is not tribal), has been an uneasy one on both sides.[71]

There is little point in disputing the generalization that Jordan evolved as a tribal society. Even Jordan's towns and villages have been dominated by tribalism for most of this century. Three major factors have contributed to change in the traditional tribal structure of Jordanian society: sedentarization, education, and communication. Any of these phenomena can be viewed as fundamentally different from the others and as either cause or effect. Because of the interactive nature of the three, each has had a distinct, significant, and relevant impact on social change.

It is clear that the effect of Israel on Jordanian life has been concrete and dramatic. Not only is this so in the sense of the Israeli challenge, which is more existential and shocking than Western penetration; it is also and potentially more so in Jordan because of the influx of Palestinian refugees in 1948 and 1967. Apart from their political challenge,

> the Palestinians brought with them to Jordan a healthy respect for modernity, knowledge and awareness of the twentieth century. Their frustration and anger [were] also accompanied by . . . hard work [and an orientation to] achievement. Politically mature, they began placing demands on the machinery of the state for services, job opportunities, facilities, and other amenities of life.[72]

It is likely, however, that even in the absence of these accelerators of change, the processes of social change would have occurred as a response to the West.

Two factors of change deserving special mention are government and change itself. First, throughout the Middle East, government has been the sponsor and mediator of change, at least in its initial stages. Many of the questions that political scientists, historians, economists, and sociologists ask about the lack of broadly based classes to introduce and mediate social change should be considered in this light, particularly as government was often the opponent of change in the West.[73] Second, it is important to recall that the rapidity and intensity of social change in countries like Jordan tend to create short-term disequilibria that in turn cause additional change. Over extended periods of time these disequilibria would have little effect, because individuals could more easily accommodate to their evolutionary appearance. But in the compressed experience of rapid social change through which Jordan is moving, change in one dimension of life (such as residence) leads to relatively immediate follow-on changes (including employment, education, association, apparel, health services, food consumption, and planning).

Sedentarization

There is no precise set of behaviors that is inclusive of degrees of sedentarization and yet representative of the full range. Sedentarization is a process, constituting an infinite range of behavioral positions. Populations may be classified as sedentary or nomadic; as sedentary, semisedentary, seminomadic, and nomadic; and so forth. There are also many causes of increased sedentarization, and in Jordan the government has encouraged the settlement process through a variety of techniques, although these means have not been as forceful as in many or most other countries of the Middle East. Nomads, loosely defined, are thought to have constituted approximately 6 percent of the kingdom's population in 1967. By the late 1970s, they amounted to less than 3 percent.[74]

The effects of sedentarization are far-reaching. Whereas nomadic populations pose almost insurmountable problems for a poor country like Jordan, in terms of providing education and other social and development services intended to create an identification with the state (as well as to serve the commonwealth), it is clear that settled tribes are much easier to reach. Settled groups also have a greater vested interest in the state than do nomads, who can move to another environment when adversity looms. (Indeed, they have done so a number of times, with substantial tribal migrations into and out of the kingdom in reaction to some policy or action of Jordan or its neighbors.) For this reason, sedentary groups are more willing to invest in their immediate and national homes – invest physically, financially, and psychologically. Settled populations tend to develop new means of cooperation and tend to redefine their concepts of community. The redefinition need not exclude old and perhaps still primary identities and associations, but may supplement those established patterns with new interactive links in accordance with new perceptions or needs and interests foreign to nomadic lifestyles.

Education

Education has a direct impact on attitudes and perceptions because it shapes the framework within which identity is conceptualized and alters the nature of social interaction at both the individual and group levels. Education provides a new range of employment opportunities and is a vehicle for government participation and influence. The distribution of educational services tends to reflect local power distribution in many areas, but the central fact is a significant growth in education opportunities across all segments of the population. Tables 1 and 2 illustrate the growth in educational experience among the bedouin tribes.

Education exposes its recipients to new ideas and approaches and provides new choices and alternatives. Over time, the new mode of thought "makes possible, indeed requires, a re-examination of all traditional relationships and structures."[75] Education is a process, and distinguishing it from indoctrination is not easy because definitions and concepts of education differ. In Jordan, as in other countries of the Middle East, the way of life associated with education and the concept underlying it (that man can improve his station in life) contribute to aspirations of social mobility and to the absorption of tangible measures of social mobility. A new set of values is acquired, and while these values may not

TABLE 1.
Educational Experience of the Jordanian Bedouin
(Percentage by Age)

	MALE				FEMALE			
Age in Years	No Education	Primary	Preparatory	Secondary & Over	No Education	Primary	Preparatory	Secondary & Over
15-19	20.4%	27.9%	36.6%	15.1%	64.8%	22.7%	11.3%	1.2%
20-24	23.5	39.6	21.5	15.4	82.0	14.4	2.7	0.9
25-29	27.2	52.5	12.6	7.7	83.9	13.5	2.4	0.2
30-34	42.8	42.3	10.7	4.2	95.1	2.8	2.1	0.0
35-39	57.2	37.6	4.4	0.8	96.7	3.3	0.0	0.0
40-44	66.1	29.9	1.8	2.2	98.0	2.0	0.0	0.0
45-49	70.7	27.2	1.6	0.5	99.0	0.0	1.0	0.0
50-54	78.3	18.8	1.5	1.4	98.0	1.0	1.0	0.0
55-59	78.7	20.0	1.3	0.0	100.0	0.0	0.0	0.0
60+	93.6	6.4	0.0	0.0	99.0	1.0	0.0	0.0
Total Population	50.9	31.6	11.6	5.0	87.6	9.1	2.9	0.4

Source: Kamel Abu Jaber et al., *Bedouins of Jordan: A People in Transition* (Amman: Royal Scientific Society Press, 1978), 43.

replace or superimpose themselves immediately on tribal mores, they do supplement and, empirically and gradually, erode the latter.

In his penetrating study of Karak, Peter Gubser notes the relative displacement of tribal identity by the sedentarized residents.[76] Although he correctly attributes the growth of other associations to many aspects of social change, it is probably a safe inference that education is more highly correlated with this phenomenon than any other single attribute. Education plants the social and economic seeds

TABLE 2.
Education and Literacy, 1952 and 1979

	1952	1979
Population	587,193	2,152,273
Students	61,500 est.	698,205
Male Students	60,000 est.	379,837
Female Students	1,500 est.	318,368
Students as part of population	10.5%	32.4%
Illiteracy	70%	29.3%*

Source: Adapted from Kamel Abu Jaber, *The Jordanians and the People of Jordan* (Amman: Royal Scientific Society Press, 1980), 109.
*1976

from which new reference groups grow and relative changes in the importance of tribal affiliation blossom. It is incontestable that this process has progressed in Jordan and has long since passed the point of no return. The debate centers on the extent of the progress.

Communication

Modern society cannot be dissociated from the far-reaching implications of mass communications, which have shaped it far more than we realize. Most major events are known in every country within hours or even minutes of their having taken place. It is difficult to estimate the impact of mass communications on our lives, but the sum of the psychological and physical effects must clearly be large.[77] Jordan, like other developing countries, is dramatically affected by the communications revolution. Kamel Abu Jaber, who supervised a major study of Jordan's bedouin population in 1978, notes that even nomadic tents have television antennas, and cassette players and transistor radios are ubiquitous.[78]

For many years, the apostles of political development have contended that communications and the government monopoly over mass communication media were among the most powerful forces in support of political integration and the development of modern nationalism.[79] We cannot deny the effect of radio and other mass media in raising the political consciousness of the Arab masses, certainly including the tribal society of Jordan. The claims must be limited, however, by several conditions. The powerful persuasive role ascribed by many observers to mass media assumes that the human mind is a *tabula rasa*. Such an observation overlooks the informal channels of communication and thought. Attitudes, opinions, and belief structures are not dependent on the mass media and are often highly resistant to even the most intensive persuasive campaigns. Indeed, communication specialists note the difficulty of changing or creating any but the most peripheral of these values.[80] People tend to develop informal networks of communication and sensitive "decoding" techniques when government-controlled mass media become powerful. By these means, they "read between the lines" and actively exchange views at variance with those sanctioned in the formal media.[81]

Moreover, it is not at all clear that these media have in fact succeeded in unifying the diverse minorities in the Arab world. There are growing indications that mass media may often be disintegrative, particularly as regards ethnic and religious minorities.[82]

In Jordan, where "East Bankers" (as contrasted with Jordanians of Palestinian extraction) are a relatively homogeneous group, there are few indications of disintegrative results flowing from modern communications, although the mass media have been used directly and indirectly by both the government and Palestinian groups to convey threats against each other.[83] Nor is there a strong indication that the mass media have, in and of themselves, significantly contributed to Jordanian nationalism in any direct sense.

By no means, however, do we suggest that the media role in tribal social change has been peripheral. One of the most powerful impulses in the empirical (as opposed to theoretical) modernization process is that of emulation.[84] The breadth and penetrative capacity of mass communication media have provided the means for this. Whether it is perceived as a force for growth, development, and constructive social change ("the revolution of rising expectations") or for impatience, discontinuity, and destructive violence ("the revolution of rising frustration"), surely there can be little doubt that emulation not only affects the present, but also provides a portrait of what the present generations (the plural is important, as generational differences must be considered) see and will act upon in the future. Emulation has, with education, been a robust explanatory variable in the sedentarization of Jordanian tribes, the nature of socioeconomic change and development, and the articulation of socioeconomic objectives at the individual level.

The Nature of Social Change and Jordanian Tribes

These three forces of change — sedentarization, education, and communications — have significantly accelerated the rate and direction of social change in Jordan. Change would have occurred in any case as a result of the presence and penetration of the West, the advent of Israel and the migration of the Palestinians, the rise of a state in the land east of the Jordan, and other factors. Clearly, we cannot say how this change "would have" manifested itself, but it is inconceivable that the speed and thrust would have been identical with what has in fact occurred.

Tribe and Government

We focus on the tribal aspect of social change because of the key role of the bedouin tribes in supporting the Hashemite monarchy in Jordan. In the Jordan Arab Army, as in the society outside the army, Jordanian tribes have been a major force for stability in the kingdom. Their role in stabilizing Jordan has not been played out only because the bedouin are conservative and oppose change. From the outset, they have identified with the Hashemites for three reasons. First, Kings Abdullah, Talal, and Hussein have enjoyed religious legitimacy by claiming descent from the prophet Muhammad. (The significance of this heritage is enhanced by Hussein's almost supernatural good fortune in surviving numerous attempts on his life.) Second, they have enjoyed institutional legitimacy as heads of state through legal processes rather than by coup or other illegal acts. Third, each of Jordan's kings has worked closely with the bedouin tribes and is viewed as a tribal leader, a kind of super *shaykh al shayukh* (paramount of the tribal shaykhs). Each of these sources of legitimacy has been an important factor in retaining tribal support.

Before considering the element of change, we should survey some of the methods used to maintain tribal support for the king and some of the uses for this loyalty.

To maintain the support of any constituency, a political leader, party, or other group must create one or more of several impressions that together constitute legitimacy. He must be perceived (1) to possess a "right" to rule based on custom, law, or morality; (2) to bear a "qualification" to rule on the basis of merit (demonstrated or expected); or (3) to provide a "return" from his rule, that is, a specific direct or indirect benefit to the group in question. To the tribes of Jordan, Abdullah and Hussein have personified *all* of these attributes. We have already considered the issue of "right" in law, religion, and custom. Their performance has generally been considered excellent, although there is a slowly increasing note of disquiet among the tribes in some areas. Finally, the benefits have been perceived as considerable. Most writers have concentrated upon the "right" to rule; having briefly discussed this consideration, we shall focus on the latter two points.

Most East Bankers take pride in Hussein's perceived Arab and world role. There is little recognition in Jordan, for example, that King Hussein's regional and global visibility has slipped in recent years and less recognition that he was much less well known and appreciated in Europe and America than his rival, the late Anwar Sadat.[85] Instead, Jordanians rightly take pride in his durability; Hussein is the senior Arab chief of state chronologically and one of the longest-tenured current chiefs of state in the world. Jordanians see in his continued reign, in Jordan's relative prosperity, and in the kingdom's stability compelling evidence of the monarch's understanding of, sensitivity to, and capable handling of the complexities of regional political dynamics. To many, or perhaps most, Jordanians, history appears to have vindicated the political style and decisions of Hussein. If Jordan has not vanquished all threats, if Jordan's policies have not always been accepted by the Arab world or Israel, still the country appears to have fared better than most. The king's East Bank subjects take great pride in Jordan's handling of the 1970 crisis, and they feel that the views and proposals of Kings Abdullah and Hussein on the Arab-Israeli problem have proven to be the best policies. They regret only that the Arab world has recognized this too late. Most Jordanians, and perhaps most nonregional observers as well, find it difficult to imagine a Jordan without Hussein. To a considerable extent, the king is more than the symbol of the state; he is its unifying essence.

Finally, there can be no question, given the close relationship of the government and the tribes, that the latter receive significant tangible and intangible benefits from the government. Tangible benefits primarily include financial support and also weapons and infrastructural development support such as land, roads, wells, clinics, and schools. Government provision of these assets has frequently been handled on a direct basis, often taking the form of direct payments—such as an envelope from the king—to tribal leaders. (These payments are increasingly seen as bribes, however, and have become a potential liability as well as a real benefit.) Payments are also provided to shaykhs from Jordanian intelligence services, the interior ministry, and the prime minister. Moreover, the army has in the past provided bounties or rewards to tribes both for recruitment and in recognition of the performance of tribe members. This system also works both ways. After coup attempts or conspiracies, suspicions, and sometimes sanctions, are leveled at tribal relatives of the plotters within the traditionally sanctioned extent of several steps removed from the culprit.

Financial and other tangible benefits are not the only means of securing or strengthening tribal support, however, and might frequently have been less important than other methods such as visits to the tribes, significant or prestigious positions for tribal members in the government, and extensive consultation on matters of mutual concern or interest. The benefits derived from this behavior vary substantially, but it must be understood that through such techniques the monarch can affect the status of the tribes vis-à-vis other sectors of society, specific tribes vis-à-vis other tribes, and groups or individuals within the tribes.

Displaying governmental and especially monarchical solicitude toward the tribes conveys messages to tribal leaders to reinforce them in their own support of the ruler, and it can also convey important messages to the Palestinians or other groups in society concerning expectations of the tribes. Thus, when problems with the PLO arise, the king ensures greater visibility for his relationship with the tribes, which he is seen as restraining. Similarly, the government has tended to give disproportionate attention to small tribes in an effort to preclude any single tribe or any small group of tribes from acquiring too much power. Thus, for example, the Majali tribe, while influential for a century in Karak, was neither large nor powerful in the whole of the country. One of the tribes promoted by the palace, the Majalis, now appear to be one of the most well-represented tribes in government. This is possible largely because it is the type and not the number of appointments that is critical – a few senior positions in the army are far more valuable than many junior positions, for example. Finally, within the tribes, the Jordanian government has used its appointments to reinforce, rather than alter, the existing social structure. Awareness of this approach helps to reinforce support for the government by the tribal leadership.

Tribalism in Jordan is on the wane. This is not to say that tribal loyalties are a thing of the past, but that tribal linkages can no longer lay exclusive claim on tribe members' allegiance. All Jordanians (East Bankers) are tribal in the sense that they can trace their descent from one or another of the hundreds of Jordanian or nearby (Syrian, Iraqi, or Arabian) tribes. Yet, for a steadily increasing number, tribal allegiance is either meaningless or peripheral to their lives and feelings. These individuals are a distinct minority in Jordanian society, generally very highly educated – at least through the college level and often to the Ph.D. – usually educated abroad, and mostly resident abroad or in Amman.

Many more Jordanians still feel the pull of tribal allegiance at times, but do not experience it as a relevant factor in their daily lives. Far more typical of the Jordanian in transition, these people are urban or semiurban (as is the vast majority of the population); at least marginally literate; engaged, even if only peripherally, in the modern economic sector; and subject to social and economic pressures that generate a growing number of outside associations, interests, activities, and hence loyalties, all of which dilute their tribal allegiance, even though it retains a considerable degree of importance. For the younger generation the tribe is strikingly less important as a symbol of identity, while for the older generation it retains substantial, and frequently preeminent, significance, at least when challenged. It will be interesting to observe the effects of aging on young, less tribally oriented Jordanians, especially whether their tribal roots gain in importance over time.

It is both too early and too simplistic to write the obituary of tribalism in Jordan, although the trend toward diminution of the significance of the tribe and of tribal power is absolutely clear. For the present generation of Jordan's key elites, however, tribal identification remains meaningful, both symbolically and behaviorally. Moreover, tribal importance will give way to more restrictive familial loyalties long before it disappears totally in favor of Western-style identities.

To explain this process some description of the structural nature of the tribe is necessary. The tribe is a pyramidal and segmentary relationship aggregating extended families into higher orders of organization based upon an "accepted myth that all living members of the tribe [are] descended patrilineally from a remote common ancestor."[86]

> The significance of the pyramidal pattern is that there is an overall vertical organization of the tribe, not just a series of horizontal units with the same general identity. But the Jordanian tribe is also inherently segmentary: each segment at each level has a separate identity

and a degree of power and authority of its own. Coupling the two concepts ... indicates that the tribe is organized in an ascending series of segments, each a political and social group at some time and in some events. Thus, each unit at a structurally higher level automatically contains all those groups below it. Nor does any real leadership hierarchy connect the groups; instead, for example, the shaykh of one of the subsections is in turn the shaykh of the section of which it is a part; similarly, the shaykh of one of the sections is shaykh of the tribe.[87]

Thus tribalism is more than a concept. Although it is certainly a set of affective perspectives and values, the relationships that are its core have an articulable and precise, though flexible, structure.

The tribal phenomenon arose as a result of identifiable environmental conditions. A facile intellectual approach is to suggest that because those conditions have changed or even disappeared, tribalism is disappearing or, more extreme, has disappeared. Social realism, however, mandates a different approach. Culture does not change quickly, as it is an aggregate phenomenon. Political, economic, and even social institutions can change abruptly, because these structures need not be rooted in popular behavior or experience, but cultural reality is much more continuous than is our analytical perception of it.

We admit, then, that tribalism is declining. The nature of the process of decline will dictate how tribalism recedes. Looking to the end of the process is at best misleading. The end point is a slice of time, no more important, though perhaps more enduring, than the infinite slices of time occurring before that point. As tribalism recedes, it does so under the pressures of proliferating associations and demands, giving way to a more restrictive definition of family. Rather than lineage, individuals will be principally concerned with smaller and more proximate familial dimensions, except to the extent that these are threatened by the tribe or that specific circumstances require reference to the larger group.

Jordan is moving from a society in which tribal association is the primary source of identification to one in which the clan or extended family, related but less comprehensive groupings, are more important and are, in fact, the primary reference group. As the tribes that remain the primary referent to their members decline, the absence of other tribes highlights a process well under way in parts of Jordan (such as the northwest) since the 1920s and 1930s. Today, few would consider most of the groups in Irbid and Salt tribes in any meaningful sense. Sedentarization, education, and increased communication affected them earlier.[88] Today we see the continuity of tribal awareness, but the importance of smaller, extended families exceeds that of tribal affiliation in most cases.[89] In the case of only an extremely small minority does the nuclear family represent the boundaries of the salient reference groups.

Thus, there is little reason to expect that tribal identification will disappear soon. Although the operational living group of the northwest of Jordan is clearly the nuclear family, and although this is common throughout most of Jordan now, it will probably take one to three generations to totally redefine the Jordanian's identity and familial terms of reference.[90]

Less clearly, but apparently, a new sense of Jordanian nationalism is growing, and social progress, economic development, political stability, and (relative) freedom are important contributors to this identity. Jordan is today in some respects what Lebanon once was – the only Arab country in which educated people feel that they can live freely and comfortably. The process of growth of a sense of national self-identity is easily misunderstood – one tends to assume that the process will continue, that a strong sense of nationhood will emerge. The outcome of the process is in reality anything but assured, however. In the early 1970s, after decades of failure in the establishment of such feelings, Syria was making strong headway toward a unified national self-concept. For a variety of reasons the process was reversed, however, and today Syria is less unified than it was in 1970.[91] It is still far too early to predict with confidence the triumph of Jordanianism, but the movement toward such national identity is certainly clear and is growing in both the traditional and the most urbanized sectors.

That a sense of Jordanian identity should emerge in Amman and other urban centers is hardly surprising. The nature of urban society, the degree of education, the growth of the Jordanian economy — all these factors contribute to an appreciation of what makes Jordan distinct among Arab countries. If the cities tend to be antimonarchical, they also tend to be politically aware, and Jordanians are conscious and justifiably proud of the role Jordan has played in the region. Moreover, city dwellers, a high proportion of whom have been Palestinian, are in the vanguard of the process by which tribal membership is becoming less important, and national identity is among the loyalties replacing that of the tribe. Whatever their views about the nature of government, the educated sector has the greatest investment and, perhaps more important, stands to lose the most from instability and disorder in Jordan, a country whose economy has been strong in recent years.

The nationalist ethos is more ambiguous among the traditional sectors. Bedouin still identify with King Hussein. Jordanian social scientists who have studied bedouin attitudes see a clear-cut movement toward the transfer of bedouin loyalty from the king to the state of Jordan. Bedouin support continues to be oriented toward the king himself, except in cases in which the East Bank character of the state is threatened. Thus, bedouin and East Bankers generally oppose the growing warmth in relations between Jordan and the PLO. They remember 1970, and, in the face of a Palestinian threat, unquestionably assert a form of East Bank nationalism. In the absence of a Palestinian threat, however, it is unclear to what extent a real Jordanian consciousness now exists among the tribes.

Some Behavioral Manifestations

It is necessary that some of the observable differences in three areas of behavior related to the process of the decline of the tribe as a reference group—physical mobility, social mobility, and social conflict and cooperation—be identified in order to reinforce the Jordanian context.

Physical Mobility. Jordan is characterized by greater physical mobility today than ever before. Operationally, this mobility must be considered from the points of view of both the tribe member and the tribe as a whole. Increasingly, people move without reference to their own or other tribal areas.[92] This results in a reduction in tribal cohesiveness as members scatter, the dilution of tribal exclusivity in tribal areas, and the effective or partial cutting off of more individuals and families from their tribal groups.

It is important not to overstate the extent to which this process has progressed. In Amman, the most advanced example of the process, there remain sections in the city still considered to "belong to" one or another tribe. Even in these areas, however, there are increasing numbers of invasions from "foreigners"—members of other kinship groups, or even new residents who have come from other countries. Other areas of the country, and even the other major cities (Zarqa, Salt, Irbid), exhibit less advanced nontribal movement and residence patterns, but the whole country is subject to these processes about which Gubser wrote as early as 1973.[93]

Social Mobility. The traditional social structure of Jordan was never dominated by class considerations, and class is still largely foreign to Jordanian society.[94] An important exception to this statement exists, however, in the form of a handful of leading families, principally East Bankers but including a few Palestinian families as well. This small aristocracy has traditionally been very closely associated with the royal family. Jordanians of bedouin descent, which in one sense or another includes virtually all East Bankers, continue to take pride in their heritage, which is, along with Islam, a great status equalizer.

Nevertheless, a middle class of entrepreneurs, professionals, and academics is developing in Jordan. Education is highly prized, and settled families endeavor to secure as much education for their children, especially their sons, as possible. This small middle class, together with Jordan's leading families, may ultimately alter the country's social structure enormously.

In the traditional sector, little has changed. The bedouin continue to disdain the peasantry, and some of the urbanites share this disdain, preferring the bedouin heritage to the image of the peasant. Most East Jordan urbanites think of their customs as bedouin and of their society as tribal in origin. Few identify in any significant way with *fellahin* customs, although tribes from Karak to Salt describe themselves as *fellahin.*

The most important change related to social mobility reflects the decline in the significance of tribal membership. Until the last two decades, opportunities to increase one's prestige or status were limited beyond the urban areas. Tribal positions of importance were largely (although never solely) based on family rank and therefore tended to be relatively rigid. The clerical sector in Jordan has never had the power or prestige it enjoyed in other countries such as Iran even under the shah.

As Jordan became a country whose population was overwhelmingly located in the cities, routes to improving status began increasingly to resemble those of the industrialized countries of the West. The sciences and professions, commerce and investment, senior positions in the civil service and academia, all became acceptable means to greater prestige and recognition in the urban sector, especially in the educated urban sector. Merit, rather than ascriptive characteristics, is becoming increasingly important in determining status.[95]

Social Conflict and Cooperation. Similarly, the nature of conflict and cooperation within Jordanian society has changed. Within the tribe, social conflict is heightened by increased social distances. Although many attributes are involved, the problem can often be seen as a generational one. Those for whom tribal allegiance is less important do not possess the same values as the tribal leadership or even their parents and grandparents, and they operate on different grounds with different objectives. It does not follow that they are uninvolved in tribal affairs, because they really are not permitted to be aloof — especially if they still reside in tribal areas — and there is competition for their support by different groups within the tribe. To the extent that they succeed in living the new style of life they prefer, they create additional conflict.

Formerly, when intratribal conflicts arose, conflict resolution was intentionally and exclusively effected within the boundaries of the tribe. Today, tribesmen, especially younger members of the tribe, increasingly look to allies outside of the tribe to influence intratribal decision-making and conflict resolution processes.[96]

As a consciousness of "Jordan" has grown, tribal members are increasingly aware of values shared with other East Bank tribes and groups on their relationship with the monarchy, some foreign policies, the role of the Palestinians, and government policies on social affairs – including tribal policies, religion, education, and development. Consequently, the tribes have been more inclined to consult as national allies and to coordinate their policies with and toward the palace.

5
Stability, Security, and Social Change

The Hashemite Kingdom of Jordan is at the heart of a turbulent region whose political dynamics—particularly those related to the Arab-Israeli conflict—place significant external and internal strains on Jordan and its policymaking apparatus. To date, the country and its government have been able to cope with these strains, but not without crisis and violence. The stability of Jordan in the face of these enormous pressures has depended upon sagacious and sensitive leadership and a firm base of legitimacy and support for the king. This chapter examines the question of how current social change is affecting, and is likely to affect, the legitimacy of the government and the stability and security of the country, both in the society as a whole and in that sector of the society so vital to the consideration of these questions—the Jordan Arab Army.

Since the establishment of the monarchy, the government of Jordan has encouraged a certain degree of social change. Some of this alteration of the existing fabric of society has affected the bedouin; some, the urbanites; and some, the *fellahin*. Although the army was a powerful agent of social change and although members of the armed forces were individually affected in significant social ways by the nature of military service and the preparation of an effective military force, the army as a social institution has been a potent agent of stability as well. In this respect, the Arab Legion and Jordan Arab Army have accurately reflected the political order that they serve, for Abdullah's concept, clearly shared by his grandson Hussein, always favored evolutionary change.

The Hashemite approach to change, or political development, should be contrasted with that of other Arab countries over the past half century. Many leaders since World War II have embraced theories or philosophies of rapid and radical socioeconomic change, and there is no need to belabor the distinction between such philosophies and those espoused and effected by the monarchy in Amman. Some governments, under substantial pressure from internal or Western sources, reluctantly adopted an evolutionary change philosophy without believing in it and sometimes without seriously attempting to carry it out. For Abdullah and Hussein, both genuinely concerned with the welfare of their subjects as well as of the state and both sensitive to the exigencies of the regional and global environment, gradual but steady and substantial modernization lay at the heart of their policies and objectives for Jordan.

The process of evolutionary change has been fundamental to the Hashemite governance of Jordan. This is a dynamic process, and at any point along the way the situation is inherently unstable, designed to be unstable enough to lead to further change, yet stable enough to resist discontinuous change. If the Jordanian social system could be isolated, as it was to some extent from 1921 to 1948, one could look with greater confidence on the ability of the government to control the processes of change. Since 1948, however, Jordan has been subject to the disruptive effects of external variables, many (but not all) related more or less directly to the Arab-

Israeli conflict, which forms the greatest threat to the process of gradual, continuous, "stable" change.

This is not to suggest that without the Arab-Israeli problem the process of social change in Jordan would proceed uneventfully — change and development are inherently destabilizing in their early stages. When the foundations of a society are subject to irresistible pressures and when the essence of society reacts to those pressures by adaptation, tremendous stresses are introduced in the lives of its people. These problems arise in addition to the difficulties encountered in their everyday lives — drought, death, sickness, and other burdens. The sterility of economic curves depicting unemployment as the economy "readjusts" must be contrasted with the realities of poverty, disease, and starvation, exacerbated by the breakdown of traditional family and tribe support practices that often accompanies modernization. These circumstances may readily lead to violence and frequently have done so. It is not only the Arab-Israeli problem that introduces violence and disorder to the area, but the sudden, violent, and disruptive character of that problem as it has affected Jordan, which stands in stark contrast with the nature and pace of change before 1948.

Decline of Tribalism

The diminished importance of tribal affiliation has had the stabilizing effect of reducing intertribal friction, which rarely exists in the modern sector. This is not to say, however, that family loyalties have disappeared or that the government is insensitive to the strength of clan and family bonds. Nepotism continues to play a significant role in the public sector in recruitment and a lesser, but still potent, role in promotion, especially to senior positions. Competition between families for many of the positions and services that the government has to offer is of a different order from intertribal feuds that existed before and exists outside of the tribal structure, because it is more clan and family-oriented with only vestiges of tribalism.

The growing independence of the individual from his tribe raises serious questions about the power of the tribe to control its members. Thus, even though the tribal shaykh supports the king, it is no longer clear that this support extends beyond the shaykh and some of the other senior elders of the tribe, and it may not be reflected in or convertible to more generalized support of the members of the tribe. In fact, the palace's payments to the tribe via the shaykhs are distasteful to many younger members, who see them as bribes. To the extent that the kingdom has looked to tribal shaykhs to maintain order within their tribes and to rally the tribes to the government in times of crisis, these changes clearly undermine the traditional foundations of Jordanian stability.

As the importance to the individual of tribal affiliation recedes, Jordan's security requirements will resemble, and be no worse than, those of other modern states. This assertion is true to the extent that the Hashemite government accurately perceives and anticipates the level of tribal cohesion. To base security on social levers that are less and less useful would be a serious error. This raises the issue of the accuracy of the Jordanian government's perceptions of social change.

It is not possible to advance a confident assessment of the accuracy of government views regarding social change and the tribes. That the senior Jordanian circles are aware of the direction and general nature of the change is, however, quite clear. Jordan University and the Royal Scientific Society (the latter chaired by Crown Prince Hassan bin Talal, brother of King Hussein), undertook a massive and systematic study of Jordan's bedouin several years ago.[97] Crown Prince Hassan paid careful attention to the findings of the research and subsequently increased his own role vis-à-vis Jordan's bedouin tribes.

If the palace is aware of the change in the strength of tribal identity, it may be asked why it continues the present policies to ensure a tribal balance in appointments and the like and provides financial and other support to the shaykhs and tribes. Yet, the existence of a change does not guarantee any specific outcome. Tribal change is a dynamic process, and at this point no one knows how much power the shaykhs have or the degree of tribal cohesion. Most observers, including most Jordanians, would readily agree that tribal power and cohesion has declined substantially, but it has not disappeared, and the decline is uneven. For example, those of the 'Adwan and the Huwaytat still living on their own tribal lands display substantial cohesion not particularly atypical of tribes that are away from Amman, geographically united, and out of government. This suffices to justify continued government and palace support.

Tribalism vs. Nationalism

What Kings Abdullah and Hussein have sought is a gradual replacement of tribal consciousness and tribal support for the king as tribal shaykh by a national consciousness and popular support for the king and government as national institutions. Although we believe such a replacement process has begun, it is important to give attention to the planned process, to the actual process, and to its implications.

From 1921 until 1948, the focal point of Jordanian nationalism was Transjordan, with its Arab people east of the Jordan River. In addition, Palestine, Syria, and Iraq were significantly more modern and urban as a whole—equally Arab, perhaps, but with less identification with the Arabian peninsula. The nationalist impulse was impeded by the lack of differentiation by border: northern Jordan might as well be southern Syria; southern Jordan, northern Arabia; eastern Jordan, western Iraq.

The events of 1948 complicated the task of identity-building because the merger of the peoples from east and west of the Jordan was never successful and detracted from the specific identity of the East Bankers or Transjordanians. Indeed, Palestinian nationalist consciousness developed earlier and was far more advanced in 1948 and thereafter, which complicated the post-1948 task of building a Jordanian identity. In 1967, the West Bank was occupied by Israel, and Palestinian national consciousness is believed to have grown even more rapidly after that.[98] If Jordan accepted the Palestinians, many Palestinians rejected Jordan, seeing it only as the necessary sanctuary and staging point from which their real home was to be regained.

If it can be said that the absorption and subsequent loss of the West Bank complicated the process of generating a Jordanian identity, it can also be suggested that the "shotgun marriage" of East and West Bankers accelerated (and perhaps somewhat perverted) the same process. The Palestinians, and especially the nascent PLO, gained strength inside Jordan and acted in ways viewed by many East Bankers as understandable but inimical to East Bank interests. Thus, Jordanian nationalism grew at least in one dimension – the development of an East Bank consciousness distrustful of the Palestinian presence in Jordan, but still sympathetic to the Palestinian cause.

Given its short history, ambiguity, and the limitations inherent in its being reactive to other countries and peoples, Jordanian nationalism is still extremely fragile. It has not replaced family and tribal loyalties, but coexists with these and other identities at varying levels of importance. Jordanian nationalism is not an enduring reality, although it has taken root among some sectors of the population, notably the urbanized, educated Jordanians, and has certainly begun to germinate elsewhere as well.

There is a feeling among some who are intimately familiar with Jordan that transference of bedouin loyalty from the person of the king as supreme shaykh to the state of Jordan has already occurred or has at least progressed very far. Most experts agree that in Amman and other urban areas, particularly among the educated, this process has already reached its final stage, and that the king is supported as the chief of state. These observations raise important questions about the stability of the country, because loyalty based upon ascriptive qualities might not be subject to the same types of changes as support based upon rational political considerations. Specifically, the king will always be the descendant of the prophet and may therefore be especially qualified to serve as supreme tribal leader, but as a head of government he may be one option among several.

The older bedouin and those in the armed forces still identify with the king on a personal level, and their loyalty to Hussein is still grounded upon this highly personalistic relationship. It would not be incorrect to say he is still seen as the supreme tribal leader, but it would be misleading. The relationship is more direct and less mediated through the tribe as an agent of legitimization, reflecting changes that have already occurred. At the same time, Jordanian nationalism has not taken firm root. That it exists cannot be denied, but it is more evident as a reaction to Palestinian nationalism and to the East Bank Jordanians' fear of Palestinian aspirations than as an assertion of positive identity. What Jordanians (East Bankers) know is that they are not Palestinians, Syrians, Saudis, or Iraqis.

Moreover, to the extent that "Jordan" is a meaningful concept, it is difficult for many Jordanians to understand that meaning without reference to the king. King Hussein symbolizes his state in a way quite unlike other rulers in the Middle East. In Egypt, Iraq, or Syria—all countries usually dominated by one man—people of the country may wonder how the death of the ruler will affect national policy, foreign affairs, orientation, or even domestic affairs, but Jordanian subjects find it difficult even to conceive of Jordan without Hussein. In Saudi Arabia, which means literally the Arabia of the Sa'ud family, as well as in the Hashemite Kingdom of Jordan, the royal family's name is part of the name of the country. Yet the contrast between the families is extreme—the large Saudi royal family is deep in leadership cadres, while the Hashemites are a small royal house with very limited alternative leadership choices. Jordan is a Hashemite kingdom in name, but Hussein's kingdom in the public mind, as it was Abdullah's kingdom before his assassination.

The personalist role of the king is clearer among cohesive rural tribes, where "Jordan" is less meaningful than tribal affiliation, and less clear in educated circles in Amman, where Jordan has tangible meaning and the king is the chief of state. Yet, even among the least sedentary and urban tribes, there is today an awareness of borders, and therefore of states, that did not exist a half-century ago. Indeed, these bedouin tribes, most of whom live or migrate near these political boundaries, are acutely sensitive to differential treatment of their tribe (and other tribes) in neighboring states. Even among these tribes, Hussein's relationship to Jordan, as well as to the tribe, is somewhat understood.

The same situation appears in the cities. Urbanites, especially the educated in Amman, think of themselves as pragmatic modernists. They are Jordanians, Hussein is their national leader, and, consequently, they support him. Few question themselves closely enough to recognize the similarities between their own concept of the king and that of the nonurban bedouin. There are major differences in conceptual structure, especially in the structure of articulated rationalization, but the behavioral profile bears some marked likenesses as well. Both share a faith in the king as a wise leader, both support Hussein against any threat, and neither can conceive of Jordan without Hussein. In fact, the most nomadic bedouin find it easier in a sense to do this, because each is less interested in Jordan and more in touch with a timeless continuity to his own lifestyle.[99]

Despite the personalist nature of urban loyalty, the growth of Jordanian nationalism and of the perception of Hussein as ruler of Jordan is clear. In crises, both of these considerations are demonstrated by support for Hussein and will continue to be so demonstrated probably for several years. Although the king's once-mystical hold over Jordan no longer applies to the most educated and urbanized sector of the population, even that sector will rally behind the king whether the threat be Israeli, U.S., Soviet, or Arab—and especially if it were Palestinian.

It is a mistake to suppose that Jordanians dislike Palestinians. Rather, there exists a legacy of fear of the Palestinians, who represent a more urbanized, more modernized, more educated, more nationalistic, and more militant people. In recent years, most educated Jordanians have concluded that the Palestinians in Jordan are not a real threat, assuming that

- the composition and structure of the Jordan Arab Army do not substantially alter;
- Syria does not seek to destabilize Jordan through the Palestinians;
- the modus vivendi with the PLO continues;
- the safety of the king is assured;
- Israel does not push whole-heartedly to destabilize Jordan;
- relative economic stability endures.

The Jordan Arab Army

The condition of the structure and recruitment patterns in the Jordan Arab Army is discussed at greater length below, because this subject is so closely related to the change of tribal roles. In spite of the broadening of the army to incorporate more Palestinians and to place them in areas previously reserved for Jordanians, it will take some years for these processes to alter fundamentally the composition and dependability of the army—if they ever do. It is too early to determine whether these changes will "Palestinianize" the army or "Jordanianize" the Palestinians.

Relations with Syria

Except for a brief period after the October War, Jordanian-Syrian relations have been characterized by a greater degree of conflict than of cooperation. Although there is a latent territorial dispute between the two countries, this has had virtually no effect on their relations for decades. Instead, Jordan's Western orientation, its strong support for an Arab-Israeli settlement, and its need to align itself with more powerful neighbors have antagonized Syria. The Western orientation has either conflicted with Syria's own reliance on the East or has prevented Syria from being the sole interlocutor with the West. Jordan's support for a regional settlement focuses on the achievement of a resolution to the Palestinian problem. Jordan has been constrained by the necessity (for economic and political reasons) for Arab world approval, but needs a settlement. Resolution of the Golan issue is not important to Jordan. Finally, the search for strong allies has often found Jordan allied with regional or extraregional partners at odds with Syria. Since 1979, for example, Jordan's principal Arab ally has been Iraq, Syria's archenemy.

The pattern of Jordanian-Syrian conflict has resulted in armed confrontation twice in recent years. In September 1970, Syrian Army units entered Jordan in support of the PLO, although Hafez al-Assad, then Syrian Air Force commander, refused to provide air cover for the Syrian tanks, which were consequently repulsed by Jordan. A decade later, in late 1980, Syrian forces again massed on Jordan's northern borders. American and Saudi diplomacy and Gulf state bribes to Syria bought a de-escalation. Syria is widely believed to be behind a terrorist campaign that has included the use of bombs in Amman and the assassination of Jordanian diplomats elsewhere.

The Syrian military threat against Jordan is real and significant.[100] At least as real is the threat that Syria might use the PLO to mobilize Palestinians in Jordan against the government. The Syrian role in supporting a new PLO leadership against Yasir Arafat in 1982 and 1983 raises the possibility that the rebels, most of whom are hard-liners vis-à-vis Jordan, might make such appeals to Palestinians in the kingdom. A number of these new military leaders previously served in the Jordan army. Similarly, hard-line Palestinian political leaders, such as George Habbash, Ahmad Jabril, and especially Nayif Hawatmah (who is himself an East Banker, not a Palestinian), are irreconcilable on the issue of Jordan and will support any move designed to unseat the Hashemites.

A Modus Vivendi with the PLO

During the brief period of Jordanian-Syrian cooperation between 1975 and 1979, Damascus sought to effect a reconciliation between the PLO and Jordan as a part of its Eastern Front strategy. Years in developing, a dialogue finally opened, but only for a short while before Jordan and Syria went their separate ways.[101] The talks were limited to elements in Fatah (the largest, wealthiest, and most influential PLO group, led by Yasir Arafat), and a new PLO role was tolerated in Jordan. Nevertheless, the Jordanian government monitored PLO activities in Jordan very carefully. Many Palestinians in Jordan, as well as East Bankers, were disturbed at this renaissance of the PLO, because they feared having to choose once again between identities.

In 1982 and 1983, King Hussein attempted to take advantage of the new situation created by the June 1982 war in Lebanon. He worked to secure a forthcoming Arab posture at the Arab summit conference at Fez in September 1982 and encouraged the PLO to move into a compromise position close to that proposed by U.S. President Ronald Reagan. After several negotiating sessions with Yasir Arafat, the king believed he had PLO assurances, only to have Arafat renege on the accord (which had been severely criticized by other PLO leaders and factions). Throughout the 1980 to 1984 period, however, the Jordanian government and the king never wholly broke contact with the moderate wing of Fatah. The split in Fatah that occurred in Lebanon in 1983 provided even stronger incentives for Jordanian support of Fatah moderates.

Israeli Destabilization

Israel is a military threat to Jordan, but many Jordanians are more concerned about the nonmilitary threat posed by Israel. The Palestinians constitute a "large half" of the population of Jordan, and many, including many Israelis, believe it is only a matter of time until the Palestinians take over Jordan. Particularly since 1977, "Jordan is Palestine" has been a favorite Israeli "solution" to the Palestinian problem.[102] Thus, when Jordanians look about them they see the possibility that both those who sympathize with and those who oppose the Palestinians could coalesce behind the idea of making Jordan the Palestinian homeland, and they note the recent increase in this "Jordan-is-the-Palestinian-state" talk.[103] Recognizing the frustration of the Palestinian people, the relatively thin Jordanian leadership cadres, and the general fragility of Jordan, Jordanians see this threat as more realistic and proximate today than at any time in the last decade – a view reinforced by history and by emigration from the West Bank into Jordan.[104] Israel is seen as a threat to the Arab world, not to Jordan alone. Thus, a primary factor in asserting Jordanian nationalism is the unity East Bankers feel against the imposition of a Palestinian state on "their" land or an attack on "their" government.

The Jordan Arab Army: Security in Change

It is important to assess how the process of social change and consequent tribal changes have affected the Jordan Arab Army, the government's views and expectations of it, and the implications for what has been perhaps the purest example of a professional and apolitical fighting force in the Middle East.

As recently as the 1970s, senior levels of the army retained much of their tribal basis. Armor, for example, continues to be dominated by bedouin officers. The army is certainly not the Desert Mobile Force, however, and change is evident in all aspects of its operations. Jordan Arab Army personnel are much better educated today than they once were, and conscription has fundamentally altered the composition of the younger officer corps. Thus, the older officers and NCOs are disproportionately bedouin, although the army has always had a reasonable number of Palestinian officers. (These latter have generally not been permitted to command strike units at the battalion level or above, however.) Key positions at senior levels — more important than numbers of personnel — have been and continue to be held by bedouin of specific tribes, often the more cohesive tribes, such as the Bani Sakhr, the Huwaytat, the Sirhan, and the Shammar.

There has been a major change in recruitment, however, that is only beginning to be reflected in the army social structure. Traditionally, many technical and support functions were performed by Palestinians because of their urban background and greater sophistication, and the bedouin officer corps was promoted through the ranks rather than recruited as officers. In the last few years, retention of qualified officer and enlisted personnel has become a major problem as far more lucrative options opened. Consequently, the conscription and promotion patterns have been forced into a new mold, giving a much greater role to Palestinians and urban Jordanians and a relatively much smaller role to tribal bedouin. Although the pattern of tribal recruitment is not believed to have changed, the proportion of recruits from nontribal sectors has been significantly altered.

Conscription was required by the need for manpower when other economic sectors were more financially attractive and by the changing nature of warfare, which has become much more dependent on technical competence and sophistication. In any case, the growing need for technical abilities would have mandated a move toward conscription at some point. Many or most Palestinians conscripted into the army do not stay in military service long, although increasing numbers (absolutely) are remaining, and the retention of these personnel, in view of the relatively diminished role of the bedouin element, will certainly affect the overall personnel structure within a few years.

The introduction of national service will also unquestionably alter the social structure and, arguably, affect the political attitudes of Jordan's armed services. Younger personnel are more sophisticated, better educated, and more cosmopolitan than their senior counterparts. They appear to be loyal to the king, as a group. What is conspicuous in its absence today, however, is not loyalty but rather the social pressure to reinforce and to stress loyalty above all other values – as well as the sensitivity to that social pressure that comes from associating one's identity and most essential needs with the peer group that demands that loyalty. This mutually reinforcing or circular set of social circumstances is only possible in a group drawn from a traditional society, such as the bedouin of some decades ago. Those who lament the change in recruitment policy overlook the substantial and continuing changes in the tribal society of Jordan, which will reduce the effectiveness of and sensitivity to social pressure.

Given the slow promotion rate that has always characterized the army and the stringent loyalty requirements of the organization, no major change in its loyalty to the king is expected in the next few years, and fundamental changes would require 10 to 15 years. For now and for the immediate future, the traditional role of the king, his charisma, and his identification with Jordanian nationalism and the Jordanian state should suffice to assure loyalty.

Short of disloyalty, however, the perspectives of army personnel with respect to the monarchy are clearly changing. As one observer noted, neither the tribes as they have moved into modern life nor their army members support the mission of the government any longer. King Hussein's religious legitimacy is still accepted, however, but is less germane to the concerns of army personnel, even of the bedouin.[105] His political legitimacy is accepted increasingly for East Bank interests—the safeguarding of the interests of historical Transjordan and the Transjordanians. Economic issues are more important to tribesmen, including those in the army, while the role of the Hashemite kingdom is of less importance. The role of "Jordan" is still to a large extent an alien concept. Thus, there may be little support for Jordanian (read, Hussein's) initiatives, but an external threat to Jordan, an internal threat to the king, or an internal threat to the political and social control of the country will engender a powerful reaction.

What can be seen is an army in the throes of relatively rapid and far-reaching social change, a process reflecting the fact that the army, especially with the national service law of 1976, is becoming a microcosm of the society at large. It will take some time, however, for the impact of this fundamental change of the armed forces to be felt in the larger society, because those entering the service in recent years, whether through conscription or otherwise, will progress slowly through the ranks and will only gradually become the majority.

Loyal to the monarch and thoroughly professional, led by officers who are zealously supportive of their king, Jordan's armed forces have maintained a history of subordination to the legal authority of the government and have established a record of noninterference in politics matched in the Arab world only by the armies of Tunisia, Saudi Arabia, and the lower Gulf countries (whose armed forces are still to some extent in their formative years). If it were possible to insulate the armed forces socially and militarily from the social change taking place in all other sectors of the kingdom, Hussein might have considered doing this, but such an insulation was never realistically feasible once Jordan attained its current level of development. Furthermore, the requirements for an effective military force have also changed dramatically and in a direction that prevents any such approach.

Some analysts have argued that "military professionalization and tribal loyalties are structurally contradictory phenomena."[106] This position reflects a Western concept of military organization and management and fails to account for the Jordanian experience. Virtually all observers have commented favorably on the fighting qualities and professionalism of Jordan's military forces. The issue is one of military change as well as social change. The nature of modern warfare has altered the essence of military organizations. Contemporary armies must be bureaucratically and technically proficient institutions. Superiority in technical competence and organization will vanquish superiority in ferocity. It is precisely the awareness of the exigencies of modern combat that have been among the important considerations in altering the nature of the army.

As the army changes, it must be considered slightly less reliable from Hussein's position. It is a more professional army and less a tribal army, bound to the king by increasingly fewer tribal loyalties—other types of loyalties might be less dependable. It will certainly be difficult for the army to maintain in its next three decades the degree of apolitical professionalism it has shown over the last three.[107] The king and the government have wisely looked ahead, however, to the possible future rather than backward to the lost past. The army they are building should be a better military force and a more professional army than it has been since 1970.

The security institutions of Jordan, particularly the Jordan Arab Army, will support the monarchy for at least the next five years, even with its mixture of new and traditional values. There is no reason to doubt that the army will defend the country at least as well in the future as it has in the past. Coups or other forms of insubordination or military intervention should not become a greater problem within the army for at least several more years, based on anticipated promotion, assignment, and rotation patterns. Even within the next few years the army could act on its own to defend East Bank interests against Palestinian encroachment in the event that large numbers of East Bankers come to feel that their interests and position are being threatened by growing Palestinian consciousness, organization, or activity.

To look beyond a single year in the Middle East is to court ridicule. Still, Jordan's prospects for stability appear no worse than those of other governments, especially as long as King Hussein is alive. The modernization of the Jordanian military will surely leave it more autonomous from the monarch, but the relationship between the two and the prospects for stability in Jordan will clearly be influenced by the course of external events as well as by the process of social change within.

6
Conclusion

The impact of social change on the role of the tribes in Jordan will be hidden, as it is being hidden now, by the velocity and magnitude of other challenges facing the kingdom — economic instability, political pincers represented by Israel and Syria, pressure to take the lead in a new attempt to achieve a peaceful settlement of the Palestinian problem, and the social divisions each of these considerations may engender within Jordan.

Although the years after Jordan's alliance with Iraq saw an economic boom in the kingdom, the boom was sustained by remittances from Jordanian expatriate workers in the Gulf and by the munificence of Hussein's Iraqi ally. As the Gulf war went badly for Iraq and the oil supply market became glutted, both sources of revenue dwindled. Whether these revenues are replaced by Saudi money or not, the problems of the Jordanian economy are clear — few natural resources, an exploding population growth, and a shortage of skilled manpower. As long as these conditions obtain — and there is no reason to anticipate change in any of them — Jordan's economic situation will remain unstable.

Political pressure from Israel and Syria will also be important. Both are military threats to Jordan, and both have used their much larger forces against the kingdom in the past. Syria has also mounted a campaign of political harassment, psychological warfare, and terrorism against Jordan and supports several groups that have frequently tried to remove the monarchy. Israeli pressure has been more subtle but no less telling. As Syria continues to oppose any Arab-Israeli settlement that its leaders believe will not secure Syrian objectives and as Israel continues to oppose any settlement that may require territorial compromise, Jordan is placed in a difficult situation. The United States, its principal arms supplier, expects King Hussein to take a forthright position that will help break the impasse, and Israel and Syria are determined to prevent such a move. There is also the question of the Palestinians in Jordan.

Each of these factors contributes to the emergence of a Jordanian national identity by existentially defining Jordanian interests and contrasting them with the interests of others. To the extent that East and West Bank attitudes diverge, however, or to the extent that they can be defined differently, a Jordanian national identity that embraces both suffers. Social attitudes and values of East Bank, bedouin-stock Jordanians are coming rapidly closer to the more sophisticated and typically urban attitudes and values of the Palestinians. But the Palestinian threat to Jordanian independence is one element in the process of national consciousness-raising, and this fact has tended to split the Jordanian nation.

The significance of tribal awareness has indeed receded, and the nomadic bedouin on whom security forces have traditionally been based have declined to the point where they constitute a negligible proportion of the population. The process of sedentarization and the impact of education and communication have wrought fundamental changes in Jordanian life, however, and have spurred the rise of new identities and loyalties that may eventually serve to undergird a true Jordanian national consciousness. These changes are particularly noticeable among the educated and urban groups.

For the present, the concept of "Jordan" is inextricably linked with King Hussein. Jordanians, whether of Palestinian or East Bank origin, find it difficult to conceive of Jordan without Hussein. The bedouin-stock East Bankers in particular love the king. Other East Bankers identify emotionally with the successes of Jordan, take pride in its heritage and role to some extent, and are also proud of their quality of life—the relative freedom and comfort of their country.

Although Jordanian identity is still a relatively nebulous concept, East Bankers see Jordan as their country and will react strongly against any threat of a Palestinian takeover as long as there is a figure around whom to rally. Indeed, the principal threat to Jordan at this time may well be that the potential Hashemite leadership perceived as legitimate is limited to the king and the crown prince. (In 1982 and 1983, the visibility of Prince Abdullah, Hussein's eldest son, was intentionally enhanced.)

The Jordanian crown prince, Hassan bin Talal, younger brother of the king, is an active, intelligent, and extraordinarily articulate asset to the monarchy. He is considered a strong Jordanian nationalist and is widely believed to favor an East Bank-only state. Hassan was an important figure in reaching the decision to use the army to restore Jordanian control over its territory in 1970 and has been an ardent advocate of both the Arab cause and, more specifically, Palestinian rights in his many articles, speeches, and books. Crown Prince Hassan is close to the tribes and the East Bank families and would certainly receive their support.

Jordanians are not concerned about a near-term Palestinian threat from within Jordan, although they are uneasy over external interest in the creation of a Palestinian state in Jordan, which they see as having support in Israel and in some quarters in the United States.

The conversion of Jordan from a rural, tribally-based monarchy to an increasingly urban modern state is progressing with new-found speed and with a degree of stability that has surprised most observers. Although vestiges of nomadic tribalism survive and although bedouin culture and tribal associations remain major — frequently, paramount — factors in individual loyalty, the transition to broader associations and more proximate definitions of identity is clear. This transition was delayed in the armed forces because of the armies' unique recruitment pattern, but is now increasingly typical there. Tribal concerns still affect the army, even though army recruitment and selection no longer reflect the former degree of tribal orientation. Still, the Jordan Arab Army seems to have been able to preserve or even augment its historic professionalism. Tight control within the army by loyal officers, as well as the genuine popularity of the king and the legitimacy of his rule, should preclude adverse changes in the supportive behavior of the security forces in the near term.

The stability of Jordan remains important to the United States. It is not so much a question of Jordan's good relations and friendship with America, nor of the Western orientation of Jordanian policy, nor of the king's earnest search for a viable Arab-Israeli settlement. In spite of its limited resources, Jordan has been an anchor of U.S. policy in the Middle East, and that anchor rests at least as much on the stability of Jordan as on the substantive policy direction of the king.

Jordan is a link between the Gulf and the Levant. This reality is political and perceptual as well as geographic. The Jordanian government's close ties with several of the small Arab Gulf states and with Oman reflect its role in the Gulf. Similarly, the dedication — a dedication that is a function of the magnitude of both threat and reality — of the Jordanians to a stable and reasonable peace on the Arab-Israeli front has certainly been a stabilizing factor in the turbulent Levant. Both these roles have been supportive of and parallel to U.S. policy. Both are even more so today.

Since the outbreak of the Iran-Iraq war, Jordan has been the most active and vociferous of Iraq's allies. Although the United States does not support either party in the conflict, there is clearly substantial concern in Washington about Iran's objectives and the implications of Iranian hegemony in the Gulf. Moreover, as destabilizing pressures have increased in the Gulf, which supplies more than half of the West's oil, political circumstances have sharply limited the extent to which any of the Arab Gulf states can be associated with the United States. In this context, Jordan's role in helping to provide security for these fragile governments while they attempt to transform their societies peacefully has been an important contribution to U.S. interests.

Meanwhile, King Hussein has worked closely with the United States to improve the possibilities of achieving an Arab-Israeli settlement. Deprived of a role by the Arab world in the decisions reached at the Rabat Arab summit in 1974, Hussein has attempted to persuade the moderates in the Fatah leadership to depart from the armed struggle rhetoric and to embark on a new strategy of negotiated settlement focusing on the West Bank. The Reagan Peace Plan of 1982 is in its general approach very similar to the king's own proposals of 1972.

In the aftermath of the 1982 war in Lebanon and the subsequent conflicts caused there by Israeli and Syrian occupation, there is some evidence to suggest that pressure will be transferred to Jordan, which serves as a buffer between Saudi Arabia and Syria and between Iraq and Israel, as well as between the Levant and the Gulf. Its pivotal position and policies supportive of stability and security have contributed to limiting turbulence and violence in a turbulent and violent region. No one seriously suggests that either Iraq or Israel, either Saudi Arabia or Syria, either the Levant or the Gulf would benefit from the loss of this buffer.

It is in this context that Jordan's internal development and its continued support for regional stability and security are important to the United States.

Notes

1. There is no adequate study of Jordanian foreign policy and relations. The only published attempt at a comprehensive study of the subject is Mohammad Ibrahim Faddah, *The Middle East in Transition: A Study of Jordan's Foreign Policy* (New York: Asia Publishing House, 1974).
2. Sidney Zion and Uri Dan, "Israel's Peace Strategy," *New York Times Magazine,* April 8, 1979, p. 21. This is, in fact, a reprise on an earlier Israeli theme. One proposal was the Reagan Peace Plan of September 1, 1982, but others included the United Arab Kingdom – King Hussein's proposed linking of a Palestinian autonomous polity of the West Bank with the Jordanian East Bank – and many others. See Avi Plascov, "A Palestinian State? Examining the Alternatives," *Adelphi Papers,* no. 163 (Spring 1981). See also Adam M. Garfinkle, "Negotiating by Proxy: Jordanian Foreign Policy and U.S. Options in the Middle East," *Orbis* 24, no. 4 (Winter 1981):847–880.

    The Rabat Conference of 1974 conferred the sole right to represent the Palestinian people (including those of the West Bank) upon the Palestine Liberation Organization (PLO). Despite the improved relationship between the Jordanian government and the PLO, developments since then, and particularly since the Camp David initiatives, have effectively reinserted Jordan into the question of representation. The Jordanian government has consistently maintained it accepts "Rabat," and therefore would only proceed to negotiate the future of the West Bank with PLO acquiescence. The Jordanian government has explored both the possibility of an Arab Summit revision of "Rabat" and the prospects of such PLO acquiescence, however, and in some cases has actively pushed for one or the other.

3. Hermann F. Eilts, "Security Considerations in the Persian Gulf," *International Security* 5, no. 2 (Fall 1980):85.

4. In 1983, the United States developed plans to support a greater air-mobile capability for Jordanian forces so that they could move to the Gulf in certain contingencies. For a variety of reasons, those Arab states whose central problem is the Arab-Israeli conflict have remained linked to Gulf Arab states. That linkage has proved extraordinarily resilient in the past, and there is no indication of any change in this condition at the present.

5. See R. D. McLaurin, ed., *The Political Role of Minority Groups in the Middle East* (New York: Praeger, 1979).

6. There is some debate as to the relative size of the two communities in Jordan today. The argument is complicated by the large number of Palestinians (and Jordanians) who have migrated to the Gulf for work. Many of these are counted as residing in both places—i.e., are double-counted. Nevertheless, we have estimated elsewhere that West Bankers are a majority on the East Bank. (McLaurin, ed., *The Political Role,* p. 274.)

7. See Nazli Choucri, "Demographic Changes in the Middle East," in *The Political Economy of the Middle East: 1973-78* (U.S. Congress, Joint Economic Committee, 96th Cong., 2nd sess., 1980), 25-55; "The New Migration in the Middle East: A Problem for Whom?" *International Migration Review,* 2, no. 4 (Winter 1977):421-433; and *Labor Transfers in the Arab World: Growing Interdependence in the Construction Sector* (Cambridge, Mass.: Center for International Studies, Massachusetts Institute of Technology, 1979).

8. Readily available and relatively accurate comparative figures are published in the International Institute for Strategic Studies' (IISS), *The Military Balance* (an annual, London). More detailed information is available in Anthony H. Cordesman, *Jor-*

danian Arms and the Middle East Balance (Washington, D.C.: Middle East Institute, 1983).

9. For a review of Jordanian military operations from a Jordanian perspective, see Brigadier S. A. el-Edroos, *The Hashemite Arab Army 1908-1979: An Appreciation and Analysis of Military Operations* (Amman: The Publishing Committee, 1980).

10. The smaller countries of the Arab Gulf area have requested Jordanian assistance in internal security—both training and operations. This is an indication of their confidence in Jordan from a political standpoint, but also of their esteem for Jordanian security services. See Cordesman, *Jordanian Arms,* Annex C, for a resumé of Jordanian security activities in the Gulf.

11. See P. J. Vatikiotis, *Politics and the Military in Jordan: A Study of the Arab Legion, 1921-1957* (New York: Praeger, 1967); Sir John Bagot Glubb ("Glubb Pasha"), *The Story of the Arab Legion* (London: Hodder and Stoughton, 1948) and *A Soldier with the Arabs* (New York: Harper, 1957); and Godfrey Lias, *Glubb's Legion* (London: Evans, 1956).

12. Kamel Abu Jaber et al., *Bedouins of Jordan: A People in Transition* (Amman: Royal Scientific Society Press, 1978), 12; Irving Kaplan, "The Society and Its Environment" in Richard F. Nyrop, ed., *Jordan: A Country Study* (Washington, D.C.: Foreign Area Studies, The American University, 1980), 63-64.

13. The Hashemite Kingdom of Jordan, National Planning Council, *Jordan Development Plan* (Amman, 1973) and *The Economic Development of Jordan (The Five Year Plan 1976-1980)* (Amman, 1975). Both discuss "equitable" and "just" distribution of the benefits of development, which, the government has indicated to the authors, means specifically the greater integration of the bedouin into national economic life.

14. It is possible to argue against the "national" credentials of any of the states of the Middle East, except possibly Egypt. Jordan's identity is particularly weak in the Levantine area, however, even by contrast with Lebanon or Syria.

The Hashemite ambitions in the Fertile Crescent area have led to the articulation of a variety of plans and actions over the last half-century. These include the "Greater Syria" concept of Hussein's grandfather, Abdullah, and the unity plans of Iraq and Jordan in the 1950s. It is unclear whether the present monarch could ever accommodate himself to the concept of Jordan as a desert shaykdom (Transjordan), although others in the royal family might be comfortable with such a role. Interestingly, Hussein retains significant properties in the Hijaz.

15. Abu Jaber et al., *Bedouins*, 43.

16. For example, tribal leaders have asserted to the authors that tribal consciousness among city dwellers who have left the tribe long before is increasing.

17. Tribal leaders have complained to the authors that the government takes the tribes for granted, that the succession is no longer carried out in Jordan (or Saudi Arabia, for that matter) in the traditional manner in which tribal leaders had a consultative role in selection of the heir apparent and the king.

18. See William F. Albright, *Archaeology of Palestine*, rev. ed. (Gloucester: Peter Smith, 1972); and G. Lankester Harding, *The Antiquities of Jordan* (New York: Crowell, 1959) for some discussion of this period.

19. This generalization must be seriously qualified. Amman, also known at various times as Rabbath-Ammon and Philadelphia, is among the oldest urban centers in the world. It lay largely abandoned for the last thousand years, however, before its rediscovery and rebirth in the late nineteenth century. Similarly, Jerash and especially Petra, which once supported 30 thousand Nabateans, have been abandoned for over a millenium as major urban areas.

20. A still-excellent history of the Arab world is Philip K. Hitti's *History of the Arabs from the Earliest Times to the Present*, 6th ed. (New York: St. Martin's, 1956). Most general books on Jordan or the Middle East also cover this period.

21. See Ibrahim Abu-Lughod, ed., *The Transformation of Palestine* (Evanston: Northwestern University Press, 1959) and other standard works on Palestine for the West Bank. For the East Bank, consider Munib al-Madi and Suleiman Musa, *Tarikh al-urdun fi al-qarn al-'ishrin* (Amman, 1959), chapter 1; and Frederick G. Peake, *A History of Jordan and Its Tribes* (Coral Gables, Fla.: University of Miami, 1958).

22. George Antonius, *The Arab Awakening: The Story of the Arab Nationalist Movement* (New York: Capricorn, 1965); C.

Ernest Dawn, *From Ottomanism to Arabism: Essays on the Origins of Arab Nationalism* (Urbana: University of Illinois, 1973); and Zeine N. Zeine, *The Emergence of Arab Nationalism with a Background Study of Arab-Turkish Relations in the Near East* (New York: Caravan, 1973) and *The Struggle for Arab Independence* (New York: Caravan, 1977) are all good, if somewhat varying, accounts of the emergence of Arab nationalism.

23. King Abdullah's account of this period is of interest (*Memoirs of King Abdullah of Transjordan* [London: Oxford University Press, 1950]), but should be read with other studies, e.g., those in the previous notes, as well as Neil Caplan, *Palestine Jewry and the Arab Question, 1917-1925* (London: Cass, 1978); J. C. Hurewitz, *Diplomacy in the Near and Middle East*, 2 vols. (Princeton, N.J.: Van Nostrand, 1956); Doreen Ingrams, ed., *Palestine Papers, 1917-1922: Seeds of Conflict* (New York: Braziller, 1973); Elie Kedourie, *In the Anglo-Arab Labyrinth: The McMahon-Hussayn Correspondence and Its Interpretations, 1914-1939* (Cambridge: Cambridge University Press, 1976); Suleiman Mousa, "A Matter of Principle: King Hussein of the Hijaz and the Arabs of Palestine," *International Journal of Middle East Studies*, 9, no. 2 (May 1978):183-194; Christopher Sykes, *Crossroads to Israel, 1917-1948* (Bloomington, Ind.: Indiana University Press, 1973); and A. L. Tibawi, *Anglo-Arab Relations and the Question of Palestine, 1914-1921* (London: Luzac, 1977). *The McMahon-Hussayn Correspondence* refers to letters exchanged between Sir Henry McMahon and Sherif Hussein between July 1915 and March 1916, in which limited British pledges to support an independent Arab state were made. The secret Franco-British agreements on the disposition of Ottoman territories are contained in an exchange of letters between the two countries on May 9 and May 15, 1916.

24. Class A mandates (those subject to Article 22[4] of the League of Nations Covenant) were deemed to

> have reached a stage of development where their existence as independent nations can be provisionally recognized subject to the rendering of administrative advice and assistance by a Mandatory until such time as they are able to stand alone. The wishes of these communities must be a principal consideration in the selection of the Mandatory.

In essence, the class A mandates (Ottoman territories) were to be guided toward an early independence. (B and C mandates were not believed to be as far along in development; their independence was not expected to be proximate.) The text of the mandate agreement is in United Nations Document A/364/ Add. 1 (September 9, 1947). Note that four years passed between the effective end of Ottoman rule (1918) and the entry into force of the mandate on Palestine (1922).

25. See al-Madi and Musa, *Tarikh,* Chapter 1, and P. J. Vatikiotis, *Politics and the Military in Jordan: A Study of the Arab Legion 1921-1957* (New York: Praeger, 1967). The mandate for Palestine was confirmed by the League of Nations Council on July 24, 1922, with an article allowing the exclusion of the application of certain articles within the mandate agreement to specific areas. This exclusion, which in effect constitutes formal separation of Transjordan from Palestine, was further approved systematically by the council on September 16, 1922.

26. The Sykes-Picot Agreement was a secret accord negotiated between the United Kingdom and France, with the approval of Czarist Russia. The relevant provisions envisaged French acquisition of the Syro-Lebanese littoral and a land area to and beyond Mosul in the east, British control of southern Mesopotamia and the Palestinian coast, internationalizaton of Palestine, and an Arab state between the British and French areas. Subsequent revisions were necessary, and of the agreement it may be most accurately said that only its general intentions and outline were applied.

27. The train was the old Hijaz Railway, and some measure of the difficulty of the journey may be gauged by noting that a distance of 1,050 km required almost a full month, with the train stopping periodically to chop down trees for fuel. See Vatikiotis, *Politics,* 42. Abdullah, *Memories,* reprints the proclamation, p. 191.

28. During this period, British policy in the Arab world was hurriedly reformulated and Faisal was given the Iraqi throne. There is surprisingly little disagreement about the political content of this meeting in the various sources.

29. Indeed, even nomadic tribes display flexible organization, units of operation varying depending upon the purpose. See C. A. O. van Nieuwenjuijze, *Sociology of the Middle East: A Stocktaking and Interpretation* (Leiden: Brill, 1971), 396.

30. The Wahhabis (after Muhammad ibn abd al-Wahhab) were religious purists aligned with the al-Saʻud family. The Saʻudis, after completing their control over the Najd, their native area (which includes Riyadh), fought a war against the Hashemites (the family of Sherif Hussein) for control of the Hijaz. The Hashemite-Saʻudi rivalry can be seen as political competition between two "houses," families, or dynasties, but much of the raiding by Wahhabi tribes, only loosely associated with and probably never completely controlled by ʻAbd al-Aziz (the Saʻudi leader), was independent of this rivalry. Undoubtedly, ʻAbd al-Aziz could have exercised greater control had there been some reason to do so, and in fact he probably "looked the other way" to a large extent — Wahhabi successes would have enlarged what was to become Saudi Arabia to include much, most, or all of Transjordan. Indeed, it is quite possible that without the intervention of British armored cars and Royal Air Force planes in the 1920s, which turned the tide against the Wahhabis, the emirate of Transjordan may have had a duration of fewer than five years. Given Britain's mandatory role, however, it did not take much to convince ʻAbd al-Aziz that Transjordan was beyond his reach and that of his Wahhabi tribal followers.

31. Although the implication of "protection" was more generalized, both parties recognized it was unlikely to be any guarantee against depredations from other tribes.

32. Although many writers, especially those of the 1920s and 1930s, portrayed this social class structure as dichotomous, it has in fact three elements: the bedouin, the *fellahin,* and the urbanized. Bedouin disdain was focused on the *fellahin* much more than on the urban population, partly because the bedouin interacted more with the former, and partly because they were more recently removed from nomadic life.

33. See A. M. Goichon, *La Jordanie réelle,* 2 vols. (Paris: de Brouwer, 1967), 2, 102, who also makes the point that Abdullah was always more oriented toward incentives than sanctions in any case.

34. Ibid., 80–81. Bulus Salman, *Khamsat ʻaʼwam fi sharqi al-urdun,* 3 vols. (Harissa: St. Paul, 1929) and M. H. Abu Hassan, *Bedouin Customary Law* (Amman: Hashemite Kingdom of Jordan, Department of Culture and Art, 1974) discuss Bedouin law and its role in Jordan.

35. Goichon, *La Jordanie réelle*, 2, 86.
36. Ibid.
37. The materials on the Palestine problem are far too numerous to list even the best here. Brief consultation of any reference work on the subject will suffice to produce an extensive bibliography.
38. John Bagot Glubb, *A Soldier With the Arabs* (New York: Harper, 1957), 26-27.
39. Despite extremely high fertility, the Arab population of Palestine actually dropped until 1950, as more Palestinians left Israel either to find a new life or to rejoin their families. This process was repeated on a much reduced scale in some of the Israeli-occupied areas after the 1967 war. See Edward E. Azar and R. D. McLaurin, "Demographic Change and Political Change: Population Pressures and Territorial Control in the Middle East," *International Interactions* 5, nos. 2 and 3 (1978):267-287.
40. See Peter Snow's biography of King Hussein for a good treatment of the relationship between Abdullah and Hussein. *Hussein: A Biography* (Washington, D.C.: Robert B. Luce, 1972).
41. A regency was required for some time so that Hussein, then in school in England, could attain the legal age constitutionally required of the monarch. The history of Jordan since the accession of Hussein bin Talal is adequately treated in many readily available sources. See Richard F. Nyrop, ed., *Jordan: A Country Study* (Washington, D.C.: Foreign Area Studies, the American University, 1980); Nasser Aruri, *Jordan: A Study in Political Development (1921-1965)* (The Hague: Nijhoff, 1972); John B. Glubb, *Syria, Lebanon, Jordan* (New York: Wallace, 1967); Peter Gubser, *Jordan: Crossroads of Middle Eastern Events* (Boulder, Colo.: Westview, 1983), chapters 5 and 6; Hussein (bin Talal), *Uneasy Lies the Head* (New York: Geis, 1962); Mishal Shaul, *West Bank/East Bank: The Palestinians in Jordan 1949-1967* (New Haven, Conn.: Yale University Press, 1978); Gerald Sparrow, *Modern Jordan* (London: Allen and Unwin, 1961); and Vatikiotis, *Politics*.
42. al-Madi and Musa, *Tarikh*, 100ff.; Vatikiotis, *Politics*, 39-40; H. St. John Philby, "Transjordan," *Journal of the Royal Central Asian Society* 24, 4 (1924):296-312; Peake, *History and Tribes of Jordan*, 106-107.
43. Vatikiotis, *Politics*, 57-58; Peake, *History*, 106; and

"Transjordan," *Journal of the Royal Central Asian Society* 26, no. 4 (July 1939):375-396.

44. The numbers and types of security forces in service in the area from 1918 until the summer of 1921, as well as their institutional relationships, are unclear. Vatikiotis is the most careful assessment of the situation, but his post facto account differs from the recollections of Abdullah and Peake, and does not agree with other historians' descriptions. In fact, no two accounts agree completely.

45. See note 42 above.

46. In May 1921 a major tribal rebellion erupted around Kura in the northern part of the territory. Al-Madi and Musa discuss it in some detail, pp. 156-164. Yet, this was only one of a number of tribal uprisings occurring in various parts of the territory. The clearest account of the agreement is Vatikiotis, *Politics,* 61.

47. Ibid., 62. The anti-Wahhabi role grew in the mid-1920s after Ibn Sa'ud's victory over the Hashemites in Arabia.

48. Ibid., 64; Peake, *History,* 108.

49. Vatikiotis, *Politics,* 70-73, gives the most candid treatment to this period. Interestingly, Peake, in his *History,* does not even mention the TJFF. He writes as if his command over Transjordan's security forces continued unrestrained until his retirement in 1939. In fact, even apart from the reduced responsibilities assigned to Transjordan's indigenous forces, the establishment of the TJFF reflected dissension within the British mandatory authority and was a symbolic movement away from the separation of the mandate into two territories, because Transjordan's security responsibilities were largely police functions, while external security responsibilities were assumed for Transjordan by Palestine (in the person of the high commissioner).

50. The role of the Royal Air Force is understandably neglected in historical accounts – "understandably," that is, in view of the authors of the accounts. Jordanians have preferred to look upon their own forces, even if commanded by Britons, as decisive in the establishment of security. The British writers on this period, while briefly but candidly describing the RAF role, have paid scant attention to it, owing to the fact that these writers have consisted largely of Peake, Glubb, their biographers, or mandatory authorities.

See Vatikiotis, *Politics*, 70ff.

51. Glubb served as Peake's deputy until the latter retired in 1939. Given Peake's views about the bedouin (see below) and the virtual independence of Glubb's force, it is not clear that he was in fact subordinate to Peake (though certainly he was in theory). Moreover, the Desert Mobile Force, under Glubb's direction and in spite of Peake's views about the bedouin, became the key element of Jordan's armed forces, while the TJFF, under Peake, was distinguished by neither success nor importance.

52. Vatikiotis, *Politics*, 73. By 1941, the Legion still totaled no more than 800 men.

The General Officer Commanding, Middle East, greatly increased the size of the Arab Legion, and used its personnel for a variety of missions during World War II. By the end of the war, the Legion had 8,000 men. World War II operations are discussed in Brigadier S. A. El-Edroos, *The Hashemite Arab Army 1908–1979: An Appreciation and Analysis of Military Operations* (Amman: The Publishing Committee, 1980), chapter 5.

Ibid., chapter 6, and Vatikiotis, *Politics*, 75–79 are the best sources. By 1950, the Legion had grown to a force of 12 thousand.

53. Vatikiotis, *Politics*, 65–68.

54. Goichon, *La Jordanie réelle*, II, 74–75.

55. To some extent, this view is misleading. Tribal experience with government authority was generally negative. Consequently, the government was viewed as a burden. At the same time, it would not be correct to portray the dominant tribal attitude as hostile. As for the bedouin, their feelings were most negative vis-à-vis the *fellahin*.

Peake's perception of the principal security threat was that bedouin violence directed against the *fellahin* and the villages would prevent imposition of central government authority and therefore the creation of a viable state. Moreover, Peake's forces, recruited from among the *fellahin* and other settled groups, tended also to view the bedouin as the principal enemy. Consequently, the interactions of Peake's forces and the bedouin were generally hostile, and by the mid to late-1920s many bedouin were fed up with Peake's forces and went out of their way to demonstrate hostility to them. Indeed, stories are recounted about bedouin attempts to humiliate Peake himself.

82   Jordan

56. Glubb, *The Story of the Arab Legion, passim.* The first triumph of the Arab Legion was changing the attitudes of the bedouin tribes, who feared central government.

The comments below concerning the representativeness of the Arab Legion in terms of tribal social structure are partially relevant to tribal representation. Recognizing the orientation of the Arab Legion to southern Transjordan, the larger tribes were reasonably represented among the troops. (The officer corps, for reasons to be discussed later, did not reflect the same pattern to the same extent, even though officers were promoted from the troops in almost all cases.) Thus, the Huwaytat, a large confederation of southern tribes, formed the backbone of the Desert Mobile Force and in the early years after merger of the various forces into the Legion, of the *jaysh al-'arabi* as a whole. Lias, *Glubb's Legion,* 65.

57. Glubb, *The Story of the Arab Legion,* 93.

58. There are several reasons for the preponderance of southern tribes. First, most of the work of the Desert Mobile Force was in the south where more intertribal conflict arose, the northern clans and tribes being more settled and the eastern less populous and "Jordanian." Second, it was a *desert* force. The northern and western part of the country were not desert. Third, the principal external threat through any desert area was in the south from the Wahhabis. Finally, and perhaps most important, northern groups were considered less loyal to Abdullah. Many were oriented toward Syria, but in other cases many simply did not relate to a Hashemite kingdom or any form of unity with the bedouin areas of the territory.

59. According to Peake, as quoted in Jarvis, *Arab Command,* 62:

> We soon saw the British Government providing money with which to subsidize tribes—the old evil of the *surra* under another name; giving them armed cars with machine-guns, wireless sets, forts, and other adjuncts to militarism, which had been denied to the old Arab Legion, who had had to carry on its task without them. This, however, would not have mattered a great deal if the Desert Force had been kept as police and not trained as an Army unit. . . .

So long as the strong hand of British retains control there is little danger in this policy, but should, in the future, a growing demand for independence be met by the withdrawal of British officers then we shall have given the tribal sheikhs an arm with which they can once again dominate the settled people, and such domination can only lead to poverty and misery. My policy was always to prevent power from getting into the hands of the tribal chiefs as the country could not prosper if this occurred.

60. Change, like stability, is a necessary element of any social system. We do not mean to suggest that social change is alien to or incompatible with Islam. Rather, we mean that Islam, which has never experienced a phenomenon like the Christian Reformation, favors tradition and resists change more than some other social systems. This characteristic must be seen as one point along a continuum, however, not as an absolute. Within every social system forces supporting and opposing change confront each other, the winner being determined by a variety of situational as well as inherent variables.

61. During the last 20 years Islam has undergone numerous interpretations favoring social change and supporting socioeconomic development. It would therefore be absurd to suggest the nonchange orientation is immutable or universally accepted. At the same time, it is also true that the modernizers tend to be more secular and less closely associated with Islam, while the clerics have for the most part opposed or criticized social changes. Although the same is true of the West, it is far less true, and society is in any event far more secular and segmented.

62. See van Nieuwenjuijze, *Sociology,* 758–760, which examines this issue carefully and historically. Van Nieuwenjuijze, however, adds that there has been a shift in thought from that of overcoming the West to that of achieving a uniquely Middle Eastern (national) self-realization (p. 760). That there is a more positive rhetorical tone to development injunctions is clear, but we feel that much of the overall absorption in development remains an attempt, however subconscious, to overcome the West. See also Kamel S. Abu Jaber, "The Dynamics of Change and Development

in Jordan," a paper presented at the Conference of the Contemporary Mediterranean World, Bellagio, Italy, August 24-28, 1981, 4-5; and Jean-Pierre Peroncel-Hugoz, *Le Radeau de Mahomet* (Paris: Lieu Commun, 1983).

63. This is not to say they have always succeeded. Sadat was killed by religious extremists. See Paul A. Jureidini, *The Themes and Appeals of Sheikh Abdul Hamid Kishk* (Alexandria, Va.: Abbott Associates, Inc., 1980), for a description and analysis of the views of one of Sadat's most potent religious critics.

64. Historically, of course, the borders of Algiers, Tunis, and Morocco were not coterminous with contemporary international boundaries. Not surprisingly, the sense of identity with the tradition of the country begins to blur as one leaves the areas historically associated with the urban centers.

65. It must be said, however, that from 1958 until about 1970 Hussein was widely seen to be protected by the United States. Even in the 1970-1971 civil war, there was a widespread belief that the United States would intervene against an external attack. Vestiges of this perception remain, but most of it was dissipated by the late 1970s.

66. The reader will observe the central role given to regional considerations and pressures in all official and unofficial Jordanian analyses of the kingdom's foreign policies. In this, Jordan resembles other weak states: its policies result less from initiative and are more often a reaction to external constraints.

67. See "Jordan: One State with Two Peoples," Chapter 9 of Daniel Lerner's classic *The Passing of Traditional Society: Modernizing the Middle East* (New York: The Free Press, 1958). This chapter remains a sensitive portrait of Jordan in the 1950s.

68. For example, distinctions between the educated and uneducated, between the urban or sedentarized and the nomadic (note that nomadic West Bank tribes existed even to 1967), between the refugees of 1948 and those of 1967, between Christian and Muslim, and between those with extensive family, clan, and tribe ties on the East Bank and those without.

69. The Arab Legion crossed the Jordan River on May 15, 1948, and captured considerable portions of the West Bank, including East Jerusalem. On April 24, 1950, those parts of the West Bank under Jordanian control were annexed to Jordan.

70. See Lerner, *The Passing,* chapter 9, or Richard F. Nyrop et al., *Area Handbook for the Hashemite kingdom of Jordan* (Washington, D.C.: The American University, Foreign Area Studies Division, 1974) or previous editions.

71. Jerusalem is a religious city of great importance for Islam. (Its Arabic name means "the holy.") Having been driven from Mecca and Medina by the Sa'udis, the Hashemites attached special meaning to their suzerainty over the Islamic holy places in Jerusalem. Abdullah was assassinated in Jerusalem, and Jerusalem is, irrespective of its pan-Islamic importance, a Palestinian city.

72. Kamel Abu Jaber, *The Jordanians and the People of Jordan* (Amman: Royal Scientific Society Press, 1980), 12.

73. Abu Jaber, "The Dynamics," 7-8.

74. Compare various editions of the *Area Handbook for the Hashemite Kingdom of Jordan* with Nyrop, *Jordan,* 64.

75. Manfred Halpern, *The Politics of Social Change in the Middle East and North Africa* (Princeton, N.J.: Princeton University Press, 1963), 29.

76. Peter Gubser, *Politics and Change in al-Karak, Jordan* (London: Oxford University Press, 1973).

77. See Lucian W. Pye, ed., *Communications and Political Development* (Princeton, N.J.: Princeton University Press, 1963) and Wilbur Schramm, *Mass Media and National Development: The Role of Information in the Developing Countries* (Stanford, Calif.: Stanford University Press, 1964).

78. Interview, October 8, 1981.

79. See Karl W. Deutsch, *Nationalism and Social Communication: An Inquiry into the Foundations of Nationality,* 2nd ed. (Cambridge, Mass.: MIT Press, 1966); Pye, ed., *Communications;* and Daniel Lerner and Wilbur Schramm, eds., *Communication and Change in the Developing Countries* (Honolulu: East-West Center Press, 1967).

80. See R. D. McLaurin, "Perceptions, Persuasion, and Power," in R. D. McLaurin, ed., *Military Propaganda* (New York: Praeger, 1982).

81. Ithiel de Sola Pool, "The Changing Soviet Union," in R. D. McLaurin, ed., *The Art and Science of Psychological Operations,* 2 vols. (Washington, D.C.: GPO for Headquarters, Department of the Army, 1976), vol. 2, pp. 1043-1050.

82. See Anthony H. Birth, "Minority Nationalist Movements and Theories of Political Integration," *World Politics* 30, no. 3 (April 1978):325-344, esp. 335-337; and Walker Connor, "Nation Building or Nation Destroying?" ibid., 24, no. 3 (April 1972):329.

Lewis W. Snider, "Minorities and Political Power," R. D. McLaurin, ed., *The Political Role of Minority Groups in the Middle East* (New York: Praeger, 1979), 250-251.

83. The nature, themes, and effectiveness of government and PLO psychological appeals are studied in Paul A. Jureidini, "The Relationship of the Palestinian Guerrilla Movement with the Government of Jordan 1967-1970," unpublished Ph.D. dissertation, The American University, Washington, D.C., 1975.

84. We are grateful to Kamel S. Abu Jaber for a useful discussion of the concept and for his use of the term "emulation."

85. Of course, any Egyptian ruler disposes of one unexcelled resource—population—because he automatically leads about 40 percent of the Arab world (Egypt's population). Size is also the Egyptian army's great strength, and therefore the ability to threaten to withdraw this army from a conflict immediately confers immense importance on any Egyptian leader.

86. Nyrop, *Jordan,* 70-71.

87. Peter A. Gubser, *Jordan,* 24.

88. Peake's *A History of Jordan* discusses and even maps the "tribes" of northwestern Jordan (pp. 143-165). His concept of tribe is slightly more flexible than that of many authorities, however, and it is not clear that tribal awareness of many groups in the Ajlun and Balqa districts was more than a very abstract phenomenon even when Peake collected his data. Moreover, his maps, which have been considered and used (even by Jordanians) as authoritative ever since the book was published, are, in fact, quite distorted.

89. See Richard Antoun, *Low-Key Politics: Local Level Leadership and Change in the Middle East* (Albany, N.Y.: State University of New York Press, 1979), 115-120.

90. See Kamel S. Abu Jaber, "The Dynamics of Change," who argues that what he calls the "cellular family," which appears to be equivalent to the nuclear family, is now the norm, excluding even the parents of the married couple (pp. 25-26).

91. R. D. McLaurin, Mohammed Mughisuddin, and Abraham R. Wagner, *Foreign Policy Making in the Middle East* (New York: Praeger, 1977), 222; Paul A. Jureidini and R. D. McLaurin, "Political Disintegration and Conflict Reduction in the Eastern Mediterranean Area," (Alexandria, Va.: Abbott Associates, Inc., SR 51, 1979).

92. Gubser, *Politics,* 120.

93. Ibid.

94. See A. K. Abu-Hilal and I. Othman, "Jordan," *Commoners, Climbers and Notables: A Sampler of Studies on Social Ranking in the Middle East* (Leiden: E. J. Brill, 1977), 142-143. Abu-Hilal and Othman divide Jordanian society into several "streams," based on access to power and defined largely by occupation. Although one cannot wholly discount this approach, it does not seem as useful as tribally-based or education-based distinctions.

95. See Abu Jaber, "The Dynamics of Change," 18-21.

96. Antoun, *Low-Key Politics,* 117-120. Antoun describes the ambivalent role of clan membership in politics in a small village in northwest Jordan. His analysis also discloses the key role of traditional clan leaders in the north or tribal leaders in the south and east in offering groups a choice of political styles and, as it may be perceived, social styles. Antoun's portrait provides a clear picture of both the inclination toward the traditional and the pressures toward the newer political-social values.

97. See Abu Jaber, et al., *Bedouins,* 14-45 for a summary of method and sample size. The results of the study have not yet been published, but exist in typescript form at the Royal Scientific Society.

98. See Yochanan Peres and Nira Yuval-Davis, "Some Observations on the Identity of the Israeli Arab," *Human Relations* 22, no. 3 (June 1969):219-233; Mark A. Tessler, "Israel's Arabs and the Palestinian Problem," *Middle East Journal* 31, no. 3 (Summer 1977):313-329; and R. D. McLaurin, ed., *The Political Role,* chapters 4 and 9.

99. Virtually everything that has been written by Westerners on Jordan stresses the loyalty of the bedouin. Authors such as Be'eri (Eliezer Be'eri, *Army Officers in Arab Politics and Society* [London: Praeger, 1970]) emphasize loyalty repeatedly. They

note that conspiracies against the king have all come from the towns, not the bedouins. Military plotters have been urbanized Jordanians. Still, bedouin loyalty is questioned by some Jordanians. According to them, the bedouin is loyal as long as he (or his tribe) is paid — and well paid. They claim that the Hashemites were ousted from Arabia by once-loyal bedouin (although 'Abd al-Aziz's forces were largely based on the non-Hashemite Najd), and resource-poor Jordan is hardly in a position to compete with Iraq, Saudi Arabia, or even Syria financially. All three of Jordan's Arab neighbors fund Jordanian tribes, not as subversive agents but for other security purposes such as control of contraband. This financial relationship gives options to the tribes and permits them a greater independence from the government than they would otherwise have.

100. See Cordesman, *Jordanian Arms*.

101. It is a characteristic theme of Syrian policy that Damascus insists on being the channel of communication and on remaining in the discussions at all times. As soon as the PLO-Jordanian dialogue began to take an independent course, the Syrian government attempted to sabotage it.

102. This point of view is particularly associated with Israel's former Defense Minister Ariel Sharon, who has expressed it forcefully to U.S. and other officials. As Abu Jaber, *The Jordanians*, 18, points out, this approach is based on an implicit myth that Jordanians (East Bankers) are too few to "count" and on the consequent assumption that it will be easier and less troublesome to deprive them of their existing state than it will be to perpetuate the absence of a Palestinian state.

103. See, for example, ibid., 17-20, which presents this concern admirably.

104. Because the subject here is Jordan we have focused on Jordanian problems and perceptions, although the Palestinians as a group are no happier with the concept that Jordan is Palestine. Indeed, an affiliation of the West Bank with Jordan — the so-called Jordanian option — is repulsive to many moderate Palestinians. See Mark A. Bruzonski's interesting article, "America's Palestinian Predicament," *International Security* 6, no. 1 (Summer 1981): 93-110.

105. Fundamentalism has been growing for some years in Jordan. Apparel and men's facial hair are easy measures, but, beyond these indicators, the rise of fundamentalism is quite clear from the well-organized religious pressures on the government. The government has not clashed openly with fundamentalists — who, in any case, are somewhat neutralized by Hussein's ancestry — but has tried to use its power of appointment to jobs to prevent fundamentalism's grasp on the population from being inescapably complete.

106. Fuad I. Khuri, "Modernizing Societies in the Middle East," in Morris Janowitz, ed., *Civil-Military Relations: Regional Perceptions* (Beverly Hills, Calif.: Sage, 1981), 169. Although Khuri explicitly includes Jordan in his comments, they seem to be directed more at Saudi Arabia.

107. See Eliezer Be'eri, *Army Officers,* and Fuad I. Khuri and Gerald Obermayer, "The Social Bases for Military Intervention in the Middle East," in Catherine McArdle Kelleher, ed., *Political-Military Systems: Comparative Perspectives* (Beverly Hills, Calif.: Sage, 1974), 55–85.

Bibliography

al-Abbadi, A. O. *Min al-Qiyam wa al-adab al-badawiyyah.* Amman: Wakalat as-Sahafa al Urdunniyah, 1976.

Abdullah ibn Husain. *Memoirs of King Abdullah of Transjordan.* London: Oxford University Press, 1950.

_____. *My Memoirs Completed (Al-Takmilah).* Translated from the Arabic by Harold W. Glidden. Washington, D.C.: American Council of Learned Societies, 1954.

Abidi, Aqil Hyder. *Jordan: A Political Study, 1948-1967.* New York: Asia Publishing House, 1965.

Abu-Hassan, Mohammed. *Bedouin Customary Law.* Amman: Hashemite Kingdom of Jordan, Department of Culture and Arts, 1974.

Abu-Hilal, A. K., and I. Othman. "Jordan," *Commoners, Climbers and Notables: A Sampler of Studies on Social Ranking in the Middle East.* Edited by C. A. O. van Nieuwenjuijze. Leiden: E. J. Brill, 1977, pp. 140-151.

Abu Jaber, Kamel S. "The Dynamics of Change and Development in Jordan." Paper presented at the Conference on the Contemporary Mediterranean World, Bellagio, Italy, August 24-28, 1981.

_____. *The Jordanians and the People of Jordan.* Amman: Royal Scientific Society Press, 1980.

―――. "Sheepland." Unpublished ms. (n.d., 1981).
Abu Jaber, Kamel et al. *Bedouins of Jordan: A People in Transition.* Amman: Royal Scientific Society Press, 1978.
Abu Jaber, Shabeeb. *Al-Mujtama' al-Urduni.* Amman: al-Sharikah al-arabiyyah li at-tiba'a wa an-nashr, 1979.
Akhiemer, Yosef. 'The Jordanization of Jordan," *Atlas* 20, no. 6 (June 1971):30-31.
Amin, Galal. *The Modernization of Poverty: A Study in the Political Economy of Growth in Nine Arab Countries.* Leiden: E. J. Brill, 1974.
Antoun, Richard T. *Arab Village: A Social Structural Study of a Transjordanian Peasant Community.* Bloomington, Ind.: Indiana University Press, 1972.
―――. "Conservatism and Change in the Village Community: A Jordanian Case Study," *Human Organization* 24, no. 4 (Spring 1965):4-10.
Antoun, Richard T. *Low-Key Politics: Local Level Leadership and Change in the Middle East.* Albany, N.Y.: State University of New York Press, 1979.
Aruri, Naseer H. *Jordan: A Study in Political Development (1921-1965).* The Hague: Martinus Nijhoff, 1972.
Asad, Talal. "The Bedouin as a Military Force: Notes on Some Aspects of Power Relations Between Nomad and Sedentary in an Historical Perspective. *The Desert and the Sown: Nomads in the Wider Society,* edited by Cynthia Nelson. Berkeley, Calif.: Institute of International Studies, University of California, 1970.
Awad, Mohammed. "Living Conditions of Nomadic, Semi-Nomadic, and Settled Tribal Groups," *Readings in Arab Middle Eastern Societies and Cultures,* edited by Abdulla M. Lutfiyya and Charles W. Churchill. The Hague: Mouton, 1970.
Azar, Edward E. *General Bibliography: Jordan Population and Economic Development.* Alexandria, Va.: Abbott Associates, 1978.
Baer, Gabriel, *Population and Society in the Arab East.* New York: Praeger, 1964.
Be'eri, Eliezer, *Army Officers in Arab Politics and Society.* New York and London: Praeger, 1970.

Bromage, T. N. "Jordan," *Journal of the Royal Central Asian Society* 49 (1962):17-22.

Bruzonski, Mark A. "America's Palestinian Predicament," *International Security* 6, no. 1 (Summer 1981):93-110.

Carr, Winifred. *Hussein's Kingdom.* London: Leslie Frewin, 1966.

Carrère d'Encausse, Hélène. "Aperçu sur le problème du nomadisme au moyen-orient," *Notes et Etudes Documentaires* 2095 (November 3, 1955).

Chatty, Dawn. "The Current Situation of the Bedouin in Syria, Jordan, and Saudi-Arabia and Their Prospects for the Future." *Nomads in a Changing World.* Philadelphia: Institute for the Study of Human Issues, 1981.

Chelhod, Joseph. "Problèmes d'éthnologie jordanienne: Nomadisme et Sédentarisation," *Objets et Mondes* 7, no. 2 (Summer 1967):85-102.

Columbia University. Bureau of Applied Social Research. *Communication and Public Opinion in Jordan.* New York: 1951.

Copeland, Paul W. *The Land and People of Jordan.* Philadelphia, Pa.: Lippincott, 1965.

Cooper, Charles, and Sidney S. Alexander. *Economic Development and Population Growth in the Middle East.* New York: American Elsevier Publishers, 1971.

Cordesman, Anthony H. *Jordanian Arms and the Middle East Balance.* Washington, D.C.: Middle East Institute, 1983.

Dann, Uriel. "The Jordanian Entity in Changing Circumstances, 1967-1973," *Occasional Papers.* Shiloah Centre, Tel Aviv University, August 1974.

──────. "Regime and Opposition in Jordan Since 1949," *Society and Political Structure in the Arab World.* Edited by Menahem Milson. New York: Humanities Press, 1973.

Dearden, Ann. *Jordan.* London: Robert Hale, 1958.

Dickson, Harold R. P. *The Arab of the Desert.* London: Allen and Unwin, 1948.

El-Edroos, Brigadier S. A. *The Hashemite Arab Army 1908-1979: An Appreciation and Analysis of Military Operations.* Amman: The Publishing Committee, 1980.

Epstein, Eliahu. "The Bedouin of Trans-Jordan: Their Social and

Economic Problems," *Journal of the Royal Central Asian Society* 25 (April 1938):228–236.

Furlonge, Geoffrey. "Jordan Today," *Royal Central Asian Society Journal* 3, no. 3 (October 1966):277–285.

Garfinkle, Adam M. "Negotiating by Proxy: Jordanian Foreign Policy and U.S. Options in the Middle East," *Orbis* 24, no. 4 (Winter 1981):847–880.

Ghawanmeh, Yusuf. *Amman Hadaratuhah wa tarikhubah*. Amman: Dar al-Liwa, 1979.

Glubb, Sir John Bagot. "Economic Situation of the Transjordan Tribes," *Journal of the Royal Central Asian Society* 25 (July 1938):448–459.

———. *Handbook of the Nomad, Semi-Nomad, Semi-Sedentary and Sedentary Tribes of Syria*, GIS (T), Headquarters, 9th Army, 1942.

———. *A Soldier with the Arabs*. New York: Harper, 1957.

———. *The Story of the Arab Legion*. London: Hodder and Stoughton, 1948.

———. *Syria, Lebanon, Jordan*. New York: Walker, 1967.

Goichon, A. M. *La Jordanie réelle*. 2 vols. Paris: Desclée de Brouwer, 1967.

Gubser, Peter. *Politics and Change in Al-Karak, Jordan*. London: Oxford, 1973.

———. *Jordan: Crossroads of Middle Eastern Events*. Boulder, Colo.: Westview, 1983.

Halpern, Manfred. *The Politics of Social Change in the Middle East and North Africa*. Princeton, N.J.: Princeton University Press, 1965.

Hammond, Paul. Y., and Sidney S. Alexander, editors, *Political Dynamics in the Middle East*. New York: American Elsevier, 1972.

Harris, George L., et al. *Jordan: Its People, Its Society, Its Culture*. New Haven: Human Relations Area Files, 1958.

Hitti, Philip K. *History of the Arabs from the Earliest Times to the Present*. Sixth edition. New York: St. Martin's, 1956.

Hussein, King of Jordan. *Mihnati Ka Malik*. Amman: Matabi ash-shairhah al-arabiyyah li al-liba'a wa an-Nashr, 1978.

_____. *Uneasy Lies the Head*. New York: Bernard Geis Associates, 1962.
Janowitz, Morris, editor, *Civil-Military Relations: Regional Perspectives*. Beverly Hills, Calif.: Sage, 1981.
Jarvis, Claude Scudamore. *Arab Command: The Biography of Lieutenant Colonel F. G. Peake Pasha*. London: Hutchinson, 1943.
Johnston, Charles. *The Brink of Jordan*. London: Hamish Hamilton, 1972.
Jones, L. W. "Rapid Population Growth in Baghdad and Amman," *Middle East Journal* 23, no. 2 (Spring 1969):209–215.
Jordan. Department of Statistics. *Analysis of the Population Statistics of Jordan*. Vol. 1, Amman: Department of Statistics Press, 1966.
_____. *Population and Internal Migration*. Amman, 1967.
Jordan. Ministry of Culture and Information. *Economic Development of Jordan, 1954–1971*. Amman: Jordanian Press Foundation, 1972.
Jordan. National Planning Council. *The Economic Development of Jordan (The Five Year Plan 1976–1980)*. n.p., 1975.
_____. *Jordan Development Plan*. Amman, 1973.
Jureidini, Paul A., and William E. Hazen. *Six Clashes: An Analysis of The Relationship Between the Palestinian Guerrilla Movement and the Governments of Jordan and Lebanon*. Kensington, Md.: American Institutes for Research, 1971.
Jureidini, Paul A., and R. D. McLaurin. *Beyond Camp David: Emerging Alignments and Leaders in the Middle East*. Syracuse, N.Y.: Syracuse University Press, 1981.
_____. "The Hashemite Kingdom of Jordan," *Lebanon in Crisis: Participants and Issues*, edited by P. Edward Haley and Lewis W. Snider. Syracuse, N.Y.: Syracuse University Press, 1979, chapter 8.
Kanovsky, Eliyahu. *The Economic Impact of the Six Day War—Israel, The Occupied Territories, Egypt, Jordan*. New York: Praeger, 1970.
Kelleher, Catherine McArdle. *Political-Military Systems: Comparative Perspectives*. Beverly Hills, Calif.: Sage, 1974.

Kirkbride, Alec. "Changes in Tribal Life in Jordan," *Man*, no. 23 (March-April 1945).
_____. *From the Wings: Amman Memoirs 1947–1951*. London: Cass, 1978.
Lancaster, William. *The Rwala Bedouin Today*. Cambridge: Cambridge University Press, 1981.
Lerner, Daniel. *The Passing of Traditional Society: Modernizing the Middle East*. New York: Free Press, 1958.
Lias, Godrey. *Glubb's Legion*. London: Evans Brothers, 1956.
Lutfiyya, Abdulla M. *Baytin, A Jordanian Village: A Study of Social Institutions and Social Change in a Folk Community*. The Hague: Mouton, 1966.
al-Madi, Munib and Suleiman Musa. *Tarikh al-'urdun fi al-qarn al-'ishrin*. Amman, 1959.
al-Majali, Haza'. *Mudhakkiraty*. n.p. (Amman?), 1960.
Mazur, Michael P. *Economic Growth and Development in Jordan*. Boulder, Colo.: Westview, 1979.
McLaurin, R. D., editor. *The Political Role of Minority Groups in the Middle East*. New York: Praeger, 1979.
Mishal, Shaul. *West Bank/East Bank: The Palestinians in Jordan, 1949–67*. New Haven, Conn.: Yale University Press, 1978.
Nelson, Bryan. *Azraq: Desert Oasis*. Athens, Ohio: Ohio University Press, 1975.
Nyrop, Richard F., editor. *Jordan: A Country Study*. Washington, D.C.: Foreign Area Studies Division, The American University, 1980.
Nyrop, Richard F., et al. *Area Handbook for the Hashemite Kingdom of Jordan*. Washington, D.C.: The American University, Foreign Area Studies Division, 1974.
Odeh, Hanna S. *The Jordan Valley*. Amman: Government Printing Office, 1968.
von Oppenheim, Max. *Die Beduinen*. 4 vols. Leipzig and Wiesbaden: Hanabowitz, 1939–1968.
Patai, Raphael. *The Kingdom of Jordan*. Princeton, N.J.: Princeton University Press, 1958.
_____. et al. *Jordan*. New Haven: Human Relations Area Files, 1957.

Peake, Frederick G. (Peake Pasha). *A History of Jordan and Its Tribes*. Coral Gables: University of Miami Press, 1958.

———. "Transjordan," *Journal of the Royal Central Asian Society* 26 (July 1939):375–396.

Philby, H. St.-John. "Transjordan," *Journal of the Royal Central Asian Society* 24 (1924):296–312.

Plascov, Avi. *The Palestinian Refugees in Jordan 1948–1957*. London: Cass, 1981.

———. "A Palestinian State? Examining the Alternatives," *Adelphi Papers*, no. 163. London: IISS, 1981.

———. "The Palestinians of Jordan's Border," *Studies in the Economic and Social History of Palestine in the Nineteenth and Twentieth Centuries*. London: Macmillan, 1981.

Qutub, Ishaq Y. "The Impact of Industrialization on Social Mobility in Jordan," *Development and Change* 1, no. 1 (1969):29–49.

Rabinovich, Itamar and Haim Shaked, editors. *From June to October: The Middle East Between 1967 and 1973*. New Brunswick, N.J.: Transaction, 1978.

Reese, Howard C. et al. *Area Handbook for the Hashemite Kingdom of Jordan*. Washington, D.C.: The American University Foreign Area Studies, 1969.

Rustow, Dankwart A. *Hussein: A Biography*. London: Berrie and Jenkins, 1972.

Salman, Bulus. *Khamsat 'a'wam fi sharqi al-urdun*. Harissa: St. Paul, 1929.

Shiber, Saba George. *Recent Arab City Growth*. Kuwait: Kuwait Government Printing Press, n.d.

Shwadran, Benjamin. *Jordan: A State of Tension*. New York: Council for Middle Eastern Affairs, 1959.

Sinai, Anne and Allen Pollack, editors. *The Hashemite Kingdom of Jordan and The West Bank: A Handbook*. New York: American Academic Association for Peace in the Middle East, 1977.

Snow, Peter. *Hussein: A Biography*. Washington, D.C.: Robert B. Luce, 1972.

Sparrow, Gerald. *Hussein of Jordan*. London: George G. Harrop, 1940.

_____. *Modern Jordan.* London: Allen and Unwin, 1961.
United Nations Economic and Social Office in Beirut. "Nomadic Populations in Selected Countries in the Middle East and Related Issues of Sedentarization and Settlement," in *Studies on Selected Development Problems in Various Countries in the Middle East, 1970.* New York: U.N., 1970, pp. 105-118.
_____. "Settlement Patterns and Problems and Related Measures and Policies in Various Countries in the Middle East," in *Studies on Selected Development Problems in Various Countries in the Middle East.* New York: U.N., 1967, pp. 31-40.
al 'uzayzi, Ruks bin Zaid. *Safahat min at-tarikh al-urduni wa min hayat al-badiyyah.* Jerusalem, 1961.
Vance, Dick and Pierre Lauer. *Hussein of Jordan: My "War" with Israel* (trans. June P. Wilson and Walter B. Michaels). New York: William Morrow, 1969.
Van Nieuwenjuijze, C. A. O. *Social Stratification and the Middle East.* Leyden: E. J. Brill, 1965.
_____. *Sociology of the Middle East: A Stocktaking and Interpretation* (Social, Economic, and Political Studies of the Middle East, I). Leiden: E. J. Brill, 1971.
Vatikiotis, P. J. "General Remarks About Research on the Military in Jordan," *Problems of Studying Military Roles in Other Cultures: A Working Conference,* edited by Ritchie P. Lowry. Washington, D.C.: The American University Center for Research in Social Systems, 1967. pp. 179-186.
_____. "Politics and the Military in Jordan," *The Military and Politics in Five Developing Nations,* edited by John P. Lovell. Washington, D.C.: The American University Center for Research in Social Systems, 1970. Chapter 3.
_____. *Politics and the Military in Jordan: A Study of the Arab Legion, 1921-1957.* New York: Praeger, 1967.
_____. "The Politics of the Fertile Crescent," *Political Dynamics of the Middle East,* edited by Paul Y. Hammond and Sidney S. Alexander. New York: American Elsevier, 1972. Chapter 7.
Weir, Shelagh. *The Bedouin.* London: World of Islam Publishing, 1976.

Yacoub, Salah M. "Sedentarization and Settlement of the Nomadic Populations in Selected Countries of the ECWA Region." Paper presented at the ninth World Congress of Sociology, August 1978.

Young, Peter. *Bedouin Command with the Arab Legion, 1921-57.* London: Cass, 1967.

NEW APPROACHES TO THE SCIENCE OF POLITICS

THE POLITICAL LIFE OF THE AMERICAN STATES
(American Political Parties & Elections, Gerald M. Pomper, general editor)
edited by **Alan Rosenthal** and **Maureen Moakley**
Although states are part of a broad national environment, politics in each state are different. This book explores the differences, which have as much to do with the distinctive political cultures of the states as they have to do with formal institutional arrangements.
344 pp. Jan. 1984 $29.95 ISBN 0-03-060327-7
Text edition: $12.95 ISBN 0-03-060328-5

SPAIN AND THE U.S. Since World War II
R. Richard Rubottom and **J. Carter Murphy**
In 1953, after five years of political maneuvering, the governments of Spain and the United States concluded the Pact of Madrid. Under the terms of the Pact, the U.S. provided Spain with economic and military assistance in exchange for limited rights to construct and use military bases on Spanish soil.
176 pp. Jan. 1984 $24.95 ISBN 0-03-069618-6

THE TRIPARTITE RELATIONSHIP Government, Foreign Investors, and Local Investors During Egypt's Economic Opening
Kate Gillespie
Here is an innovative study of the tripartite relationship among government, foreign investors and local private investors. In particular, the author examines Egypt during its economic opening under Sadat, although the implications of the study are more far-reaching. The author contends that there are discernible patterns of coalition building and erosion among the three parties concerned with foreign direct investment in developing countries, and that they tend to enter into bipartite coalitions that are often short lived, as each of the parties tries to maximize its own advantage.
254 pp. Feb. 1984 $28.95 ISBN 0-03-069559-7

HAITI: POLITICAL FAILURES, CULTURAL SUCCESSES
(Politics in Latin America, A Hoover Institution Series)
Brian Weinstein and **Aaron Segal**
This detailed volume presents and analyzes the two worlds of Haiti: one, the rural masses from whom have emerged an original and vibrant culture, and two, the urban-based elites who have saddled the land with an immobile political order unwilling to tackle the enormous economic and social problems the country has faced from independence in 1804 to the present day.
192 pp. Feb. 1984 $25.95 ISBN 0-03-069869-3

GEOPOLITICS OF THE CARIBBEAN
(Politics in Latin America, A Hoover Institution Series)
Thomas D. Anderson
This detailed study examines conditions in the small island states of Latin America in the context of the geopolitical factors and relationships of the entire Gulf/Caribbean Basin. The book emphasizes the special circumstances that confront the newly independent ministates in regions of larger power interests.
192 pp. March 1984 $27.95 ISBN 0-03-070553-3

U.S. INFORMATION AGENCY
Public Diplomacy in the Computer Age
Allen C. Hansen
Provides an inside and detailed view of how the U.S. public diplomacy machinery operates through an expert analysis of the history, policy, and potentiality of the U.S. Information Agency.
270 pp. March 1984 $29.95 ISBN 0-03-063286-2

THE WINNING TICKET
Slatemaking in Daley's Illinois
(American Political Parties & Elections, Gerald M. Pomper, general editor)
Melvin A. Kahn and **Frances Majors**, both of Wichita State University, Kansas
The Winning Ticket describes the role of the most tightly controlled 1960s political organization in the U.S.—the Cook County Democratic Central Committee. The book closely studies the intricate working of the Cook machine in the nominating process, and uses it as a model through which to better understand leader-controlled nominations.
304 pp. March 1984 $29.95 ISBN 0-03-069298-9

FOREIGN POLICY DECISION MAKING Perception, Cognition and Artificial Intelligence
(New Dimensions in International Studies Series)
edited by **Donald Sylvan** and **Steve Chan**
A compendium of important contributions to contemporary foreign policy decision-making literature. Includes analyses from the fields of psychology and cognitive science, as well as from political science.
360 pp. March 1984 $28.95 ISBN 0-03-069771-9

Available through your local bookseller, or order directly from:

PUBLISHERS
521 Fifth Avenue New York, N.Y. 10175

THE WORLD, AND YOU

Now In Paperback
THE CONDUCT OF A JUST AND LIMITED WAR
William V. O'Brien, Georgetown University

"A comprehensive and well-reasoned analysis of the Catholic Church's doctrine of the 'just war,' especially as it can be applied to the limited-war situations and policies of recent years. Korea, Vietnam and Yom Kippur are treated as case studies."
— Foreign Affairs

"...O'Brien is to be applauded for inviting a dialogue between the moral philosopher and the military strategist and for demonstrating areas where common discourse might prove productive."
— American Journal of International Law

510 pp.	1981	$43.95	ISBN 0-03-059346-8
Paper edition:		$15.95	ISBN 0-03-069743-3

GLOBAL PERSPECTIVES ON ARMS CONTROL
edited by Adam M. Garfinkle
(FOREIGN POLICY ISSUES: A FOREIGN POLICY RESEARCH INSTITUTE SERIES)

Provides an international perspective on the crucial issues of contemporary arms control. William R. Van Cleave, a well-known U.S. conservative, and Genrikh Trofimenko of the Soviet Institute of the U.S.A. and Canada respectively elaborate the superpowers' policies in this area. There follow essays from prominent European and Asian analysts expressing the concerns of their countries. This important compendium is drawn from the Seventh International Arms Control Symposium held in Philadelphia, May 1982.

ca. 176 pp.	1983	ca. $25.95	ISBN 0-03-069658-5

THE NEUTRON BOMB CONTROVERSY:
A Study in Alliance Politics
Sherri L. Wasserman

176 pp.	October 1983	$21.95	ISBN 0-03-064154-3

US INFORMATION AGENCY:
Public Diplomacy in the Computer Age
Allen C. Hansen

ca. 176 pp.	April 1984	ca. $22.95	ISBN 0-03-063286-2

THE WINNING TICKET:
Daley, the Chicago Machine, and Illinois Politics
Melvin A. Kahn and Frances J. Majors

ca. 256 pp.	January 1984	ca. $25.95	ISBN 0-03-069298-9